Successful Non-Fiction Writing

A guide to getting published

NICHOLAS CORDER

First published in 2006 by
The Crowood Press Ltd
Ramsbury, Marlborough
Wiltshire SN8 2HR

www.crowood.com

British Library Cataloguing-in-Publication Data
A catalogue record for this book is available from the British
Library.

ISBN   1 86126 855 6
EAN   978 1 86126 855 6

Typeset by SR Nova Pvt Ltd., Bangalore, India

Printed and bound in Great Britain by Biddles Ltd, King's Lynn

CONTENTS

INTRODUCTION – WHY CHOOSE NON-FICTION?

Every now and again, some unknown writer hits the headlines. He or she has just been paid an enormous sum for what is sure to be a blockbuster novel. Writing fiction suddenly looks like the path to riches beyond our wildest dreams.

News like this distorts the reality of the writer's lot. True, there is a small band of extremely wealthy novelists, whose every book is guaranteed to hit the best-seller list. These folk appear to have the statutory manor house in the Home Counties, a stylish loft apartment in New York and a small chateau on the Riviera. But this tiny band is easily outweighed by the vast majority of fiction writers who barely scrape an income from their writing; many aren't even able to write full-time, holding down a day job whilst scribbling in the evenings. Poets have it harder still. Short-story writers are often limited to a handful of women's magazines and competitions (most of which charge an entry fee).

Nevertheless, each year thousands of perfectly intelligent people cast their hats into the writers' ring in an attempt to become published authors. They spend years producing novels that will never get further than a publisher's slush pile and devote hours to producing short stories that will never see the faintest slick of printer's ink. Writing imaginative works is a hard business: your chances of long-term, sustained success are slim. Getting a play produced, a novel into print, a film made or your sitcom on the box is difficult. Even placing the occasional short story with a supermarket magazine requires talent, perseverance and a mixture of luck and timing.

Writing non-fiction is a practical alternative. It is highly unlikely that you'll ever become part of the jet set, although you may occasionally rub shoulders with them, but at least you will be producing work that stands a chance of publication. More importantly, most non-fiction writers can make a steady income, and so could you (even if you aren't going to have private bankers beating a path to your door).

Non-fiction may be the less glamorous sister of fiction, but she does get to go to the ball, and far more often. Of the 100,000-plus books published in the UK each year, around 75 per cent are non-fiction. True, when you go to your local bookshop all the tables and shelves at the front will be taken up with the latest fiction titles, but beyond this you will see that books on education, travel, sport, self-help, reference works, computing, DIY, cookery, gardening and so on take up a vast amount of the shelving. Similarly, you only have to browse the magazine racks in your local supermarket to see that there are probably 1,000 articles for every short story printed. Non-fiction is big business and there is no reason why you can't be a part of it.

This book is aimed at helping you to write saleable non-fiction. It is not for seasoned journalists but for the outsider, with his or her nose pressed up to the publisher's window, wondering how to break into print. The book is not intended to be a self-contained writing course, although it does contain examples and exercises. Obviously, if you want to write, then you will be trying to put into practice some of the suggestions in the book. Be warned, writing exercises are just that – exercises – they are not the real thing. It also covers a lot of ground, and whilst I hope it is full of practical advice, it can't go into huge detail about every single aspect of non-fiction writing.

You must, as you read, decide what areas of writing interest you. By all means concentrate on what is important to you, but keep an open mind. Often, what you learn about one area of writing can be applied to others – writing a press release that will catch an editor's eye is not a million miles away from writing a pitch to sell an article, for instance. It is also important to decide what you don't want to write as well as what you do. Whatever your thoughts, I would not try reading the whole book in one sitting; some of the ideas need time for reflection. Nor do you have to read it in order. I have laid it out in the order that I think is logical, but what I consider logical may not be what you consider logical; read it in whatever way suits you best.

Good luck! I hope that what you sell at least makes buying this book, and the time spent reading it, worthwhile.

Nicholas Corder

1 THINKING LIKE A PROFESSIONAL WRITER

WHAT MAKES A NON-FICTION WRITER?

Many people dream of turning the spare room into a study, buying the latest computer wizardry and from the safety of their little room banging out works of astonishing genius that are snapped up by editors and publishers. The reality is somewhat duller. You can bankrupt yourself with the best in IT, have the world's largest spare room (with built-in sauna, jacuzzi and gleaming stainless steel cappuccino-making equipment), but there is still no guarantee that you are going to make it as a writer.

However, there are certain things that you can do to increase your chances of success. Much of this book is concerned with these techniques, but before we get to the nitty-gritty of writing, there are a few basic questions worth considering.

Do You Enjoy Writing?

Do you like dealing with words? Setting them down on paper? Do you like poring over what you've written and rewriting what you've done to make it the best you can? And can you do that regularly, without waiting for the Muse to strike?

If you don't enjoy writing, you'll soon get bored and find something else to do. To put it bluntly, if you want to succeed as a professional writer, even on a part-time basis (or perhaps, especially on a part-time basis with all the other pressures of home, work and family), then you have to get down to some hard graft.

Do You Have Self-Discipline and Sticking Power?

There is a well-worn quotation, attributed to dozens of different writers from across the years: in answer to the question 'Where do you get your inspiration?' comes the reply, 'I'm inspired every day at 9 o'clock when I sit at my desk.' Often would-be writers dismiss this as being 'all right for a full-time writer, but I've got a job'. There is an element of truth in that, but most full-time writers got to be full-time by displaying self-discipline as part-time writers. Busy people usually find time to get things done; determined people get things done come what may.

You can have all the talent, ideas, flair for words and industry contacts in the world, but if you're not prepared to put in the time at your desk, then you won't get anywhere. As a professional relying on freelance non-fiction writing for all or part of your income, you can't afford the luxury of waiting for inspiration to strike. You have to be writing those articles, sending out those ideas or hacking your way through a rough first draft of a book.

You don't have the excuse of 'writer's block' either. You have a blank piece of paper (or screen) and you must get words onto it and, if you are going to make any money, you need to get them to your editor or publisher by a predetermined date or you've just broken your side of the deal and may not get paid.

Can You Set Yourself Deadlines?

Managing your time is essential, especially when you start out and probably have a lot of competing pressures. Deadlines are the key; most of us are hopeless without one. I was once asked for a piece and then told 'No hurry ... whenever.' It took me a year to come up with 1,200 words. Frankly, if I had been asked for it by lunchtime, I could have done it. It might not have been the best piece ever written – but it would have been finished.

Working to a deadline is easy. The difficulty when you're starting out is that there are no deadlines to speak of, so the trick is to create imaginary ones. No one needs that article by Friday, but if you've got a first draft written by then, you have achieved something.

For some of us, the difficulty in finding the time to write is that we fritter away so much of our time on other activities. I often give new writers the advice to try to find half an hour every day to get some writing done. If you do that, and can manage to produce 250 words in half an hour, then after four days, you have a 1,000-word article.

Some people would prefer to work in larger chunks of time less often, but this is not always possible. Often, it seems hardest for women with family commitments to make the time to write. It is hardly surprising when there are the demands of children and the household to be met. There is also the constant nagging guilt that many mothers feel if they aren't doing something for their family. However, if Joanne Rowling managed to write *Harry Potter* whilst coping with a new baby, then there is no reason why you can't find the odd half an hour here and there to try your hand at a short article. Explain that you are doing something for yourself, and if you can find somewhere to escape, so much the better.

Do You Like Dealing with Facts, Opinions and Ideas?

An enquiring mind is probably the greatest attribute you can have if you want to write non-fiction. You need to be open to a wide range of ideas and opinions, some of which you won't necessarily agree with, if you are to come up with saleable work:

- Do you buy a new gadget and then find yourself fascinated by how it works and have the need to take off the cover?
- When politicians trot out a series of statistics, do you ask where they got them and if they actually mean anything?
- Do you marvel at the way your small child acquires speech?
- Do you wonder what goes on behind the doors of an abattoir?
- Can you imagine what it must be like to live full-time in a caravan?
- Do you wonder what happens to footballers from lower divisions when they retire from the game?

Are You Capable of Working by Yourself?

One of the hardest parts of being a writer is that it is an antisocial activity. Yes, you may get out of the house to interview people and you probably get to meet, or at least speak to, some interesting folk. However, there are days when you might not speak to a soul outside your own family. This can be difficult if you are not by nature a solitary person. On the other hand, if you are happy with your own company, then what better life could there be?

What all this boils down to is that you have to ask yourself not only if you are cut out to be a non-fiction writer, but 'how' cut out you are. For many people, being a part-time professional writer is enough. It enables them to bring in some extra income by doing something they enjoy, but they are not dependent on it for their entire livelihoods.

However, it doesn't matter whether you aim to be a part-time writer knocking out the occasional feature every few months or so, or intend to devote every waking hour to freelance writing. The route to any kind of success involves professionalism: you would expect a part-time dentist to look after you just as well as one who worked full-time.

DON'T LET ME PUT YOU OFF

Despite the drawbacks, writing non-fiction is great. Assuming you have some facility with language, you have only to sit down and get on with it. If you have got time to watch TV, you have got time to hack out a few hundred words a day. Add in some determination and a little perseverance and you could soon be making an extra income from your writing. It may not be a fortune, but it could pay for holidays, put the children through university or boost your pension. You might even be one of the lucky ones who is able, eventually, to give up your job and devote yourself to writing full-time.

Writing non-fiction also has a huge advantage over writing fiction in that you can often find out if a publisher or magazine editor wants your work before you have actually written it. The typical first-time novelist will spend years beavering away on their manuscript in the evenings and at weekends. When they have finished it, it will do the round of publishers until, if they're lucky, someone offers them a small sum to publish it. Few succeed.

Non-fiction books do not sell in the same way. I hadn't written a word of this book before I signed the contract; I sold the *idea* of this book. I had thought about the various topics to include, had done some research to see what similar books were available and had done a great deal of the spadework for the book, having taught courses in writing non-fiction. However, what I hadn't done was spend every free moment of my waking life working on a project that might not see the light of day. You will read in Chapter 7 how to go about selling a book. Similarly, it is rare that I write a complete article without having pre-sold it.

In a nutshell then, writing non-fiction is both economical in terms of your time and with such high levels of demand it is easier to break into. But don't think that writing non-fiction isn't creative. It may not require the flights of fancy that fiction demands, but you only have to look at the travel section of any bookshop to see just how well-written a great deal of non-fiction can be. Besides, if you want to write fiction, it isn't going to harm your reputation if you can show a prospective agent or publisher that you have some kind of track record. Writing a 100,000-word novel pulled from your own imagination is not the same as writing a non-fiction book of 50,000 words that you have been able to research at your local library. However, much of the craft and all of the discipline are interchangeable; many writers of fiction have backgrounds in journalism, where they learnt the skills that have stood them in good stead. Writers as varied in their styles as George Orwell, Jilly Cooper, Keith Waterhouse and Bill Bryson are or were all time-served journalists.

There are plenty of positive aspects to writing for a living. On the upside:

- You work your own hours.
- You get to see your name in print.
- You don't have to sit in traffic jams too often.
- Your travel-to-work time is often a matter of seconds as you pad down the hall to the spare bedroom.
- You have picked a cheap trade – there is little in the way of specialist equipment needed to be a writer.
- You get to read a lot, and writers like reading.
- Writers have kudos, for some unknown reason (even if they rarely have cash).
- You get to drink as much coffee as the human body can take.
- As an English-speaking writer, you have a world-wide market at your finger-tips.

However, writing isn't all tea, crumpets and lavender-scented handkerchiefs. On the downside:

- You are unlikely to make a fortune.
- Most of your friends don't think you have a proper job.
- Everyone thinks they can interrupt you at any time of the day so that you can go and house/baby/cat-sit for them.

- No matter how hard you try, there are some days when you just can't get going.
- In some office-based jobs, you can hide behind the in-tray for an hour until you can face the day.
- There is no pay cheque at the end of every month.
- You're working for yourself now: self-discipline is paramount and you have to rely on yourself to do nearly everything associated with your business.

There is also often a sense of precariousness about writing for money. When you go full-time, you are always figuratively knocking on doors and asking if anyone will buy your wares. As Arnold Bennett once said, 'A freelance writer is a tramp touting for odd jobs.'

So, don't become a writer if:

- Making money is more important to you than job satisfaction.
- You can't take criticism or rejection.
- You have no desire to know more about subjects that may not be immediately appealing.
- You don't enjoy reading.
- You easily get lonely/distracted/caffeine poisoning or miss the chat around the water cooler.

Above all, don't become a writer for the fame and fortune. You are more likely to be set upon by a transvestite gorilla in a public park than you are to find yourself garlanded with praise and a bulging wallet. There's one simple rule – only write if you want to.

2 Ideas, Ideas, Ideas

Ideas are the lifeblood of any writer. This is as true for the writer of non-fiction as it is for anyone embarking on a piece of imaginative writing. Before starting on any kind of writing you need to have some notion of the subject(s) about which you are going to write. Those who complain of 'writer's block' probably sit down with a blank screen or piece of paper in front of them and have no idea. If you always have some idea – no matter how vague – you should at least be able to make a start on a piece of writing.

So where do writers find their ideas? It is a question we writers are often asked and in some ways it is difficult to answer. People who have ideas continue to have ideas. They probably can't quite put their finger on the process, but they know that they are on constant idea-alert and are receptive to them when they do come across them.

There is nothing terribly clever about finding ideas, yet it can often be the hardest part for a writer who is starting out. Ideas are all around us – they are ours for the taking. They are simply there waiting to be plucked out of the ether and used. However, most of us overlook them. I suspect that this is because we are all looking for the *big idea*; the one that has never occurred to anyone else ever before, the one that will change the way the world thinks.

You don't need a *big idea*. You're not out to discover a new Theory of Relativity, you are looking for material for articles and books. You're not trying to write a PhD thesis – something that involves several years of intensive original research – you are simply looking for something that could form the basis of an article. If you're lucky, you might stumble across something that could build into a series of articles or even a book, but to begin with, simply coming up with ideas for articles is fine. As you begin to open your eyes and ears to possibilities around you, you will soon see that you will have plenty of material.

From Your Own Life

Perhaps one of the best ways to start is by mining your own life. All of us have a mixture of experiences: good, bad and lukewarm. We have jobs and families (or if we don't, we can write about *not* having them). We know people from different walks of life. We have medical problems, hobbies and responsibilities.

We cook food, tend the garden, fix the car and put up shelves. We have pets. We have all had some kind of education (and that Physics A level that seemed such a waste at the time might just come in handy now as you think how you might explain how a certain gizmo works for a popular science magazine).

We may not have swum the English Channel, won Olympic Gold or routed the Australians with devastating spin bowling but we all have a raft of experience and knowledge. Our everyday lives are full of rich experiences; all that experience and knowledge can be put to use producing non-fiction.

Let us imagine that you've spent the last ten years teaching primary school children. You may not consider yourself an expert within the academic discipline of education itself. However, to anyone outside education, an expert is exactly what you are. You have a ready source of material; you have that precious store of experience and knowledge that would be of great use for a more general readership. Parenting magazines, for instance, would be an obvious target market and without even straining for ideas and with minimal research you could come up with pieces on:

- How to help your child to read.
- How to help your child with arithmetic.
- Good books for your child.
- How much should you help your child with homework.
- Do we ask too much/little of our children?
- How to handle parents' evenings.
- What does the latest educational jargon mean?
- What your child should be able to do on the computer by the age of ten.
- Which musical instrument best suits your child.
- If it is worth paying for extra tuition.
- Out-of-school activities that would help your child's development.

I am sure that you could add plenty more ideas of your own to this list: try the same exercise with your own job.

OTHER PEOPLE

Writing about other people can be a tricky area. You often see intrusive articles about people's lives in magazines. Often these tell the tales of people who have coped with drugs, sexual misconduct, family problems, crime or disaster. You probably don't want to alienate your friends by exposing their darkest secrets to the public, but they can still be a source of useful information.

A friend has developed late-onset diabetes. Another has returned to university as a full-time mature student. An ageing relative has to move into a rest home. All these are potential sources of ideas. You do not even have to write about the person involved; they are simply the source of the idea.

Nor do you have to rely simply on your friends. A well-known writer is coming to give a reading at your local book store – can you arrange an interview that you could sell to a relevant publication? If they are a children's writer, perhaps you could sell a feature to an educational magazine? If the writer is well-known for specializing in a particular topic, could you sell to a relevant hobbyist magazine? The writer's latest novel deals with the subject of a child with dyslexia – could this be the kernel of an idea for a parenting magazine?

LOOK AT THE MARKET

You can also work backwards. If you come across a magazine – perhaps one that is new to you – you can ask yourself the simple question 'What can I sell them?' I have often found this to be a useful way of coming up with ideas. Loitering in a large newsagent, browsing the shelves will often be the trigger-point of an idea for an article.

One good rule of thumb is to think 'the same but different'. If a magazine recently carried a feature about parents raising a child with Asperger's syndrome, they are highly unlikely to want another piece on the same issue. However, they might well be interested in a piece about families dealing with similar difficulties.

LOOKING FOR GAPS

Sometimes you don't even have to come up with a completely different angle. For instance, many publishers have lists that cover the same sort of ground. It is often worth obtaining relevant publishers' catalogues and comparing what they have on offer. Sometimes you will see that Publisher A has a book on a certain topic, but Publisher B does not. Now, there may be a good reason for that; Publisher B might not think that there is enough demand for that book. They might also have one in the pipeline, being prepared by an author who already writes for them. However, it looks like an opportunity, so might be worth a try.

Sometimes gaps are even more obvious. When a new series comes out, it has to be built up. A publisher has started producing a series of county guides entitled 'Activities for Children in ...'. You notice that the publisher doesn't cover the county where you live. It is an obvious gap, so it may be worth approaching them with a well-written book proposal (*see* Chapter 8).

NOTHING NEW UNDER THE SUN

Another good method of sourcing ideas is simply to take an idea from one source and apply it to another. An article in the travel section of an upmarket Sunday newspaper about staying in luxury hotels in the Loire Valley would hardly sell to *Camping World* or *Budget Backpacker*. However, an article using the same basic premise – the holiday in the Loire – might well sell to the camping magazine if you slant it towards staying under canvas. *Budget Backpacker* could also be interested in a piece if you could tell the reader how to wangle rooms in five-star hotels for a couple of pounds a night.

KEEPING AN IDEAS BOOK

Contrary to popular opinion, not all writers keep a notebook. I suspect they are the exception, rather than the rule however – perhaps they have better memories than most of us.

There is no secret as to how to record your ideas. Any writer who tells you there is only one way to keep notes and records is selling snake oil. The best method is the method that suits you. You might be happy with a cardboard box into which you stick your random jottings; you might keep some kind of computerized record.

However, I do recommend keeping some kind of system just for your ideas. I use an A4-size exercise book at home and try to carry some kind of smaller notebook at all times. I also have a small, inexpensive voice recorder that I can keep in a top pocket. If anything strikes me, I can jot it down (or record it) and then transfer it into the larger book when I get home. I use an A4 book so that I can expand the idea and have space to jot down some potential markets using a double-page spread.

At this stage, I try not to worry about whether or not the idea is any good. Sometimes, you can tell straight away that you are onto something. At other times, what seems like a great idea fizzles out and comes to nothing. Similarly, sometimes when you flick through your ideas book you come across ideas that didn't inspire you at the time and suddenly, you see a different slant.

Essentially the more ideas you have, the more good ones you will find amongst them. True, you will probably have a lot of duds, but that's not the point. Nobody ever has to see your truly awful ideas. Put it this way: which writer is better off? The one who has one brilliant idea, but for some reason just can't sell it, or the writer who has a hundred ideas, ninety-five of which are duds, but five of which she sells?

OTHER TECHNIQUES FOR GENERATING IDEAS

Brainstorming

This is a particularly useful technique for a writer. Sometimes 'brainstorming' is also known as 'word-showering'. Simply take a piece of paper and write down a key word at the top. Then write down any other words that occur to you that might be associated with that word.

The important thing with brainstorming is that you shouldn't think too hard; just let the words flow. Whatever you do, do not pass any critical judgements on your ideas until you have a good, full page of scrawl in front of you. If you try to filter out the bad ideas, you can end up filtering out the good ones

Brainstorming example: Motor Caravanning in France

Where?	*When?*	*Types of ferries/crossings*
Distances		*Tourist spots* *Off the beaten track*
Cost comparisons		*Types of sites Facilities on sites*
Wild camping	*Who goes* *Culture*	*Coast vs. Inland*
Good tips for first timers		*Taking your pets – vaccinations etc*
Speaking the language		*Key words and phrases* *Insurance*
Motor caravan check before you go		*Breakdown cover*
What to take What to buy		*Cost of fuel What to do with kids*
Specialist stuff – chateaux, vineyards, fruit picking, horses		
Farm sites Route planning		*Weather/temperatures*
Pitfalls Driving in France	*Areas to avoid*	*Motorways*
Museums Cost of living	*Eating out Personal safety*	
Specialist equipment – triangle, bulb kit, headlight deflectors		

As you can see, the list is neither organized nor complete, but at least it is a way of getting down plenty of ideas.

as well. For the time being, you just want to get them down on paper. Don't worry about the order in which they occur to you, just get them on the page. Later you can cast a cold, critical eye over your jottings.

Mind-Mapping

Mind-mapping is a more sophisticated version of brainstorming. Essentially it is a way of writing down ideas as they occur to you, whilst fitting them into some overall pattern. By writing ideas in a list, you can give the impression that the first item on your list is more important than one halfway down, whereas we all know that that is often not the case.

Mind-mapping involves writing your main subject matter in the centre of a piece of paper and branching out into a series of main points. These in turn can be sub-divided into minor points. The beauty of a mind-map is that you can add things to it as they occur to you.

There are several advantages to using mind-mapping techniques over the traditional method of linear note-taking. The main areas of your thinking are clearly defined. We also have some idea of the relative importance of ideas, with the more important ideas being nearer the middle. You can also make links between the different concepts and change them without worrying too much about how it all looks, because if the drawing gets too messy you can easily start again.

Arrows are a useful way of indicating how the various ideas interconnect and of making those links immediately recognizable. You can also use colour and different shapes (circles, squares, triangles) and sizes of boxes. So, for instance, you could have your main ideas in blue boxes and your subsidiary ideas in red circles.

There is a course I run called 'Writing Feature Articles', and I include here a mind-map that I use for it. See how the arrows indicate links: for instance,

16

the arrows between 'The Market' and 'Ideas' go in both directions. My thinking behind this was that you can get ideas from looking at the market but you also need to see if there is a market for your ideas.

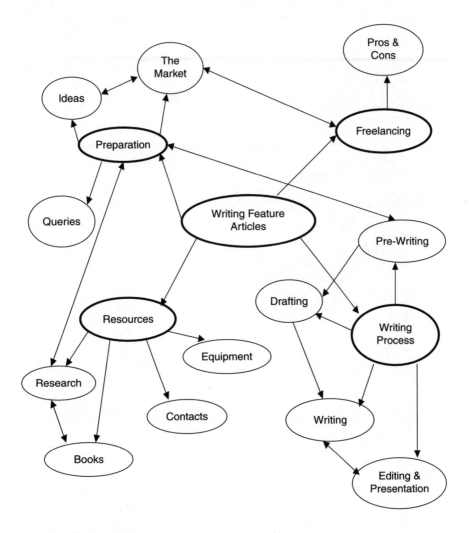

Don't worry if my mind-map doesn't make total sense to you, it is primarily meant as an aid for me.

Exercise: Developing Ideas

For each of the following series of questions you will need a clean sheet of paper. Give each sheet a heading – Work, Family, Hobbies and Friends. Start thinking about your life. Don't worry about trying to think in an orderly fashion, just ask yourself some of the following questions and jot down possibilities as they occur to you (scribbles are fine). If you come up with other ideas that don't seem to fit these headings, simply grab new pieces of paper.

Work

- What jobs have you had?
- What did you have to do?
- What skills did you need?
- Would you recommend the job?
- What advice would you give to anyone starting that job?
- Have you any good anecdotes?
- Do you know anyone who left the job and became rich or famous or both?
- Are there trade magazines that you know of, about which 99.9 per cent of freelance writers would not have heard?

Family

- What are your experiences of marriage?
- Childbirth?
- Raising children?
- Paying for children to go to school or university?
- Have you overcome family difficulties?
- Have you coped with diseases or disasters?
- Where do you go on holiday?
- Where have you lived?

Hobbies

- What do you do with your spare time?
- What do you enjoy?
- Do you have any tips?
- Do you know an expert in the field whom you could interview?
- How do you do a particular aspect of the hobby?
- Is it unusual for women/men to be involved?
- Are there fairs/rallies/exhibitions?

Friends

- Do any of your friends have unusual jobs?
- Are any of them well-known?
- Do any of them suffer from an unusual disease (you don't have to get too personal – you are looking for ideas, not exposés)?
- Do they have particular skills or talents?
- Do they have children who have developed particular skills and talents?

When you have done this, take a look at what you have written. Is there anything here that might make an article, a series of articles, or even a book? If there is anything that looks even remotely promising, transfer it into your ideas book. If there is anything that fills you with enthusiasm, then start writing about it straight away.

3 SMALL ACORNS, MIGHTY OAKS

Pick up almost any magazine or newspaper and you will see that in amongst the longer pieces, there are smaller items. Snippets of news, quotations, overheard conversations, something cute said by a child, an interesting or unusual fact or a silly sign all come into this category. They, along with such items as jokes, puzzles, handy hints, crosswords and the like are often referred to as 'fillers'. Sometimes, these fillers will have their own page; in other publications they will be dotted about as light relief.

One way of testing yourself against the market is to write them. Some writers have used this as a springboard to greater success. In fact, some teachers of non-fiction writing reckon that this is the best way to start out. I don't agree: whilst there is certainly some skill in fillers (especially in compiling crosswords), concentrating on them too much could deflect you from greater goals.

However, I do think that there are certain aspects of the filler that are useful to you as a writer:

- Fillers can give you confidence: a well-written letter to the editor that sees its way into print can help to give you a boost.
- They are (usually) quick to produce.
- They often pay disproportionately well.
- Prizes are generally tax-free and often the value of the prize is better than the equivalent payment for an article.
- You can often use them again at a later stage – it is the form of words that is copyrighted, not the idea itself.
- It can get you known to an editor.
- Writing fillers does not prevent you from writing other things.

If you have slightly loftier ambitions for your writing, you might see fillers as just one potential adjunct to what you do. If you have no ambitions whatsoever in this direction, then simply skip to the next chapter.

LETTERS

Magazines usually like to have a dialogue with their readers and they do this partly through their Letters page. Almost every magazine has a Letters page, and most importantly for you, many offer prizes. Flicking through a pile of assorted magazines in my study, I found that in addition to some straightforward cash payments that varied from £5–50, a published letter could win me any of the following: an old-fashioned tea caddy with tea; a mobile phone; a coffee-table book about Britain; a set of three camping directories; a bouquet of flowers; some golf balls; a set of watercolour paints; a china dog; a satellite navigation system; a day in a health spa; a posh ballpoint pen; a pedometer and a cafétière set.

Now, many of these things may not be on your wish list, but they might make decent presents. And don't think that you are fobbing off your friends and relatives with freebies: it is your skill that won the prize and there's no real difference between that and using your skills to earn the money to buy them in the first place. At worst, you have got something for the PTA raffle or when a charity calls at your door.

You need to read a couple of issues of the magazine to see what the editor goes for. Do they like praise for the magazine, references to previous articles, something controversial or do letters contain advice for other readers? Once you have established this then you can write something appropriate.

Unfortunately, there is no guarantee that your letter will be published, so you are chancing your arm a little. Nonetheless, it has the advantage of testing what you've written to see if it is the kind of piece the editor might want to see appearing in their pages.

COMPETITIONS

There are so many competitions out there, and not just in magazines, that a whole industry has sprung up around the subject. There are some people who do very nicely out of them. Styling themselves 'compers', they approach the task of winning competitions with professional zeal. It is hardly surprising, when there are so many luxury goods out there to be won. Serious compers spend their lives buying exactly the right packets of soap powder and breakfast cereal to get the coupons they need; I have a suspicion that some spend just as much time working at competitions as they would at a proper job. But then, on the other hand, where's the fun in having a proper job?

There are other competitions that you might find more taxing than the typical sloganeering. For instance, *The Spectator* has a regular competition slot in which entrants are asked to write in a certain style or address certain topics. Whilst the prizes are in the order £20–30 and won't make you rich, and often you are expected to write a poem, which is not the domain of non-fiction writing, you might find them useful for getting yourself in the right frame of mind. Competitions have strict rules and deadlines – just like the world of non-fiction writing; they can be fun to do and they get you thinking about writing. If you have had an idea buzzing about in your head all week, then they are helping you to think like a writer.

THE THINGS PEOPLE SAY

One popular filler item is the gaffe. These are sometimes *faux pas* by famous people; at other times, they are overheard snippets of conversation. The magazine *Private Eye*, for instance, pays £10 a time for 'Colemanballs', which consist of well-known commentators (normally sports reporters) being quoted as saying stupid things. 'The World Cup happens every four years, so it's going to be a perennial problem', from the lips of Gary Lineker, once won me a tenner.

However, it is not just gaffes that interest magazines. A lot of them like the short, humorous anecdote. *Reader's Digest* is one of the best-known and highest-paying markets for these. Sections such as 'Laughter – the Best Medicine' require only a couple of lines. However, as in all writing, the fewer the words, the more each word counts. If you are sending in an anecdote make sure that:

- It is likely to be what the magazine wants – an anecdote about a teenager is of little use to a magazine called *You and Your Toddler*.
- It is humorous – we all want to smile and laugh – and humorous with a moral is even better.
- It has a beginning, a middle and an end, just like any other story.

JOKES

I am constantly amazed at some of the old chestnuts that appear in magazines; it seems to me that there must be a market for recycling old gags. As it is the wording of jokes that is copyrighted and not the joke itself, then I suppose there is nothing other than a sense of pride to stop you from buying up every joke book from every charity shop and rewriting the gags in them.

The majority of jokes used tend to be either squeaky clean, or if they do venture towards anything that might be considered unseemly are more likely to be of the Donald McGill/George Formby innuendo level than they are top-shelf men's magazine. It's not a bad idea if you are sending out jokes to send a page of linked jokes around a theme – for instance, ghost jokes for Halloween or kitchen jokes for a cookery magazine. Don't expect to have the BBC breathing down your neck inviting you to write a sitcom, but you might make a few bob.

VISUAL GAGS

There are plenty of magazines who print the visual equivalent of the gaffe, such as misprints from newspapers ('canal holiday' advertised as 'anal holiday') or signs from abroad where words may be spelled the same but don't have the same connotation – 'Vomit Café'.

Of course, you cannot simply invent these gags, but if you get into the habit of photographing signs when you see them, or snipping misprints from the newspaper and sending them off, then you are developing good reflexes as a non-fiction author. You are beginning to look for material.

GREETINGS CARDS

Although few greetings cards fall under the category of non-fiction, if you come across humorous items, then you may be able to sell the idea to a greetings card company if they are presented in the correct format. You don't need to be able to draw or write poetry.

If you have an idea, often it will be in the form of a joke which is set up on the outside of the birthday card (page 1), with the punchline on the inside page (page 3). Your submission should be typed on one sheet of paper and would (apart from the fact that this particular joke is so old you'd never sell it) look something like this:

Page 1:   Picture of a pile of money
               Words 'You look like a million dollars ...'
Page 3:   Words 'All green and crinkly.'

Again, check out the card companies to see if they take unsolicited material, and if they do, get into the relevant shops to see what kind of cards they are looking for – some are vulgar, others more restrained.

RECIPES

Many of the recipes that you see in magazines are provided by staff writers, so opportunities are not necessarily all that thick on the ground. You need to come up with some original ideas and also often to think in terms of themes, such as: recipes for a children's party; for a summer barbecue; for an old-fashioned afternoon tea; seven things to do with windfall apples; alternatives to sugar for diabetics.

Whilst it might be tempting to rewrite a recipe by a well-known chef and pass it off as your own, you are likely to be breaching their copyright. Your best option is to use a recipe that has been handed down through the family, or to adapt traditional recipes to give them a new twist.

Cookery is one of the most popular topics in magazines. Some call for one-off recipes, but if you are looking to develop a career as a specialist cookery writer, then you need to look for a niche or a gimmick. Are there magazines that do not currently print recipes, but might? Student magazines, for instance, might be interested in recipes for meals that are cheap but nutritious. Are there particular foods that are good for arthritis sufferers/diabetics/nursing mothers? There are magazines aimed at all of these types of people. You will also come across the 'send us your recipes and win a toaster'-type competitions and these are possibly an excellent way for you to try out your ideas.

HANDY HINTS

For years *Viz* comic has published beautiful parodies of the handy hints that are often found in women's magazines. Their suggestions have included such gems as putting the goldfish in the freezer before moving house (so as to prevent spillage) and changing your name to that of your car registration number (in order to save money buying a cherished number plate). Whilst it is easy to mock these little tips (some of them deserve it) some handy hints are in fact exactly that – handy. The best hints are a little offbeat without being so far-fetched that they enter the realm of the *Viz* spoof.

SEASONAL ITEMS

Times of the year such as Christmas, New Year, Guy Fawkes Night, Halloween, Easter, summer and winter solstice bring with them a slew of related items. Editors are often inundated with articles on these subjects, so it is sometimes harder to sell seasonal material than you might expect. On the other hand, it is a good time to get in some smaller items: 'Five things you never knew about Guy Fawkes', 'Seven tips on dealing with winter blues', 'Easy recipes for a New Year's Eve party without serving cold turkey'. These items are often needed as much as six months in advance.

REVIEWS

These are an excellent way of building up a collection of clips. There is a steady demand for reviews of: art shows and exhibitions; books; concerts; films; plays, both amateur and professional; restaurants; tourist attractions. There may be little financial reward in reviewing, but you do get copies of books and to see plays and shows for free. The main advantage for you is that you can quickly build up a portfolio of articles that will be useful elsewhere.

It helps to know something about your subject before you start. Often reviews are a good way of getting in with the local newspaper. The best approach is by writing a covering letter, introducing yourself in the briefest terms, stating what you would like to review and including a sample review. Make sure that you have checked out the newspaper or magazine to see what the typical length is; there is no point in sending a 1,000-word critique of a novel to a magazine that prints only 100-word reviews.

SENDING OFF YOUR FILLER

Most filler items should be printed double-spaced on a single sheet of paper. Write your name and contact details, single-spaced, in the top right-hand corner and include a short covering letter. Many magazines are happy to receive fillers by email. If they are, follow the magazine's guidelines for this; if not, put the words 'Idea for filler' or 'Filler' in the subject line of your email message. Give the magazine nine months to use your item, unless it is genuinely topical. If they haven't used it by then, send the idea elsewhere.

To Sum Up

Many fillers are written in-house and it is probably best to regard them as either a try-out for something more substantial or as an occasional adjunct to larger projects. The advantage of fillers is that an editor can often slip them in – they don't take up the space that a feature article would take and so can often be published quickly. Sometimes ten or twenty minutes' work can bring disproportionate reward.

It is easy to dismiss fillers as fluff. Often they are, but then what's wrong with fluff? You can also dismiss them as 'not real writing'. This is only partially true; you have to write fillers in the same way as you write any other non-fiction. However, it is probably not the actual writing of fillers that will be useful to you in the longer term; of more use is the fact that you are now beginning to examine magazines in detail. You are already developing the good habit of looking for potential markets; a skill that is vital if you are to sell articles and books, which we will look at in the next few chapters.

4 WRITING ARTICLES – WHAT SHALL I WRITE AND WHO MIGHT BUY IT?

Writing articles is the bread-and-butter work of many non-fiction writers. There is a huge number of magazines out there, most of which need contributions from freelance writers.

If you're not convinced, just visit your nearest large newsagent. Even in my small town, the newsagent's shelves bulge with magazines covering a vast range of subjects – music, yachting, camping, hairstyles, home improvements, cookery, wine, disability issues, parenting, women's interests, 'lads' mags', regional interests, climbing, religion, education, computing, motorcycling, celebrity lifestyles, farming ... you name it. Also, if it isn't there, they can probably order it for you. Even the most esoteric of subjects seem to have their magazines; to the best of my knowledge there are at least four magazines devoted to the subject of tattooing.

Then look for the magazines that take short stories. There are only a handful and they probably print at least five or six non-fiction pieces for every story. The market for 'factual' writing is much greater than it is for short stories, poetry and other creative forms.

So why not sell them what they want? True, some of these magazines will be written entirely by salaried editorial staff. However, employing staff is an expensive business, so many magazines are heavily reliant on outside contributions, even if they do have some staff writers. After all, they do not have to pay the office accommodation costs, National Insurance, sick pay, pension contributions and crèche fees of freelance writers. Even when they pay us decent sums for our work, we are a comparatively cheap way of providing 'copy'. So, if these magazines need freelance contributions, why can't you be one of the people who provides them?

START SMALL, WORK YOUR WAY UP, BUT DON'T WORK FOR NOTHING

As a rule of thumb, the greater a magazine's circulation the more they pay. Many of the biggest magazines buy their copy from well-established freelancers who have earned their spurs and come from a professional journalism background. Whilst it is not impossible to break into these more lucrative markets, competition is fierce and it is more realistic to have less lofty ambitions. You're probably best aiming your early work at the smaller, hobbyist publications. They may not pay particularly well, but you can build up relationships with them and they are not always inundated (although there are surprising exceptions).

Some smaller magazines rely heavily on contributions from their readers. These are often non-professional writers who have built up so much experience in the hobby that their wobbly prose is forgiven. A well-written article that is a cut above their average offering may soon find a home.

Some magazines would love to be provided with their material free of charge (although they would soon see a deterioration in quality). It may be tempting to accept no payment just to see your name in print, but you are doing yourself and others long-term financial harm. If you are happy not to be paid for your writing then stick to the Letters column and leave the rest of the magazine to those of us who want to make ends meet. In fact, if you write for free, you are essentially stealing food from the professional writer's table.

WHERE DO I FIND OUT ABOUT MAGAZINES?

There are two main handbooks in the UK. The *Writers' and Artists' Yearbook* and *The Writer's Handbook* are both published annually and are readily available from most bookshops. They provide useful information about several hundred magazines that can be bought in the UK. There is also an equivalent publication for the USA and Canada called *Writer's Market*, which is more detailed than its British counterparts. Because it serves an entire continent, you will find that it covers, possibly, a wider range of subject matter than similar publications in the UK.

However, none of these publications covers the entire range of magazines and newspapers in print at any one time. Likewise, even the largest newsagent in the UK stocks only a fraction of the magazines and newspapers available. The market is much larger than you might imagine.

There are also thousands of trade publications, foreign magazines, local/regional/national newspapers (both free and for sale), listings and promotional material that most of us do not know about, but all of which need articles (if not always from freelancers). Your nearest decent-sized library may have a copy of *Willings Press Guide*, which is much more comprehensive than either of the guides for writers. For a view into another world, just spend an hour flicking through its pages.

NEWSPAPERS

Selling to newspapers is rather a different process. Because newspapers are usually published on a daily or weekly basis the topicality of what they want means that any copy you supply dates quickly. A magazine article is often not time-bound in the same way; it doesn't matter whether or not the article is published now or in six months.

Newspaper editors need to know that you can deliver them what they want on time. You should pitch your work to newspapers by telephoning the appropriate editor; in the case of your local newspaper this might be the named editor of the paper. In the case of larger-circulation newspapers, there could be different editors for different areas – arts, sports, politics, whatever.

If you keep your eyes and ears open, you may find local stories that could be of interest to the national press, for example a murder, a political scandal or a celebrity visit. But you are more likely to be able to sell a national newspaper the information than a finished article. Selling to newspapers is hard unless you have a track record as a journalist.

That said, there are sometimes possibilities with local newspapers, even if the pay is not always tremendous. If you fancy reporting on your local football team or writing reviews of theatre plays then there is no reason why you shouldn't approach an editor. To do this, work out how long a relevant piece would be and submit a couple of examples, together with a covering letter explaining what you are looking for.

Don't expect to make a lot of money this way, though. Often, you will receive little payment save for free entrance to the events in question. On the other hand, it gets you known at your local paper and could also be the source of work in other ways, whilst helping you to develop a portfolio of work. Besides, you never know, you might get a big star at your local theatre and be able to sell an interview to a high-paying magazine.

Your market is, therefore, most likely to be magazines, so it is worth reading as many of them as possible to get a feel for what editors require. You will also find that there is another side effect from doing all this reading – it will give you ideas for articles of your own.

Studying a Magazine

You can learn a great deal from a magazine just by flicking through it. By taking a mildly scientific approach to what is in its pages you can glean even more. Writers' guides might give you an outline, but they are no substitute for proper research. As a rule of thumb, you should read at least three copies of a magazine before pitching to it.

Adverts

First of all, take a look at the adverts. How many of them are there? If it is a serious journal there may be very few. A consumer magazine may carry hundreds. How large are these advertisements? Who is advertising? Is it mainly large corporations with household names, specialist companies, or smaller firms and individuals? How expensive are the items in the adverts – are we talking Lambrusco, Lambretta or Lamborghini? Look at the people in the advertisements. What age are they?

Advertisers spend a great deal of time and money researching exactly the best places to advertise, so they have a good idea of who buys the magazine. If a magazine is advertising walking aids and arthritis cures it is probably aimed at a different market to one that advertises lager and shaving cream. These are stereotypes, of course, but as you read more and more magazines you will become aware of the subtle differences between two or three publications that initially look and sound similar.

Letters

Another useful guide to magazine readership is to check out who writes to the magazine. Do the correspondents use their first names or formal titles? What is in their letters? How articulate are they? Do they state the obvious or come up with new and original ideas? How complex is the language they use?

Articles

There are two aspects of articles that you need to look at. First, think about the actual content. Are there are any themes that crop up time after time? Are they heavily anecdotal or do the writers look to deal with ideas? Is the content difficult or simple (or even simplistic)? Second, you need to look at the level of language being used. What is the typical length of a sentence, a paragraph or an article? What kind of titles do they use? Are there any techniques that the writers use to grab your attention early on in the piece?

Pictures

In the same way that you can tell a great deal from the adverts, you can also draw a number of conclusions from the pictures in a magazine. What kinds of pictures does the magazine use? Do they look like pictures that have been taken deliberately to support the article or ones that might simply have been supplied by a tourist board or photographic library? What is the style of the pictures? Is there as much emphasis on the photographs as there is on the articles themselves?

The Readership

You should now have a fair idea of the people who read this magazine. If you want to take your research a little further you can now go and stand in the newsagent and check out who actually buys the magazine. How old are they? Can you guess what their level of education is? What kind of social class do they belong to? Is it just one sex who buys the magazine? Why do you think they buy that particular magazine and not the similar one right next to it?

Media Pack

Getting hold of an advertisers' pack (which is sometimes known as a media pack) is a good idea. You can get one by contacting a magazine's advertising department. A well-organized media pack will give you plenty of details, including a profile of the readership – their age, sex, household income and so forth – exactly the kind of information that will make it easier for you to target that particular magazine.

Word Count

Lastly, if the information is not available in one of the writers' guides, do a word count of the articles in each magazine to see what the typical length is. Don't forget that this might vary from one section of the magazine to another.

WHAT KIND OF ARTICLE SHALL I WRITE?

There are as many different types of article as there are people under the sun. Trying to pigeon-hole an article into a certain category is difficult and probably not worthwhile, although being aware that there are several types of commonly published article is useful. The categories below are not exhaustive, but hopefully, they will get you thinking about the different kinds of approaches you can take.

How-To

Hobbyist, specialist and women's magazines are full of how-to articles. These might range from a series of recipes to an explanation of how to build a scale model railway. Simple pieces based on sociological and/or psychological issues such as 'How to deal with an unruly teenager' or 'Amusing your toddlers on long car journeys' are essentially how-to articles. A quick browse along the newsagent's shelves will soon reveal that the how-to is used extensively by many different magazines.

How-to articles are surprisingly difficult to write. They are not about launching into high-flown descriptions or for showing off your verbal dexterity, they are concerned with explaining to the reader the processes involved in a certain project.

If you have a hobby or have skills that you can share with others, then it is well worth considering this kind of article. It is also helpful if you are used to teaching people, so if, for instance, you teach cake decorating in an adult education centre and can express yourself clearly and precisely, then this could stand you in very good stead. A skilled cake decorator selling an article on, for instance, making a 'Treasure Island' cake, will probably also need to be able to supply photographs of the various stages of the process (*see* Chapter 10).

Unless you are at the forefront of a new craft, hobby or psychological trend, you probably won't make your fortune from how-to articles. However, there is such a massive demand for them from all sorts of magazines that they are not to be ignored as a good source of steady income.

Humour

The difficulty with humour is that it is a matter of personal taste. What has one person rolling on the floor, clutching their sides and demanding emergency oxygen leaves another cold. There are few magazines nowadays that are completely devoted to humour and most are written in-house or by in-the-know contributors or celebrities, so there is little scope for the outsider.

As humour varies widely, it is worth thinking about the kind of age and social group to whom your sense of humour is going to appeal. Jokes that refer to Vera Lynn, Tommy Trinder and rationing will mean little to the MTV generation. Similarly, an upmarket magazine stuffed full of pictures of country homes and Chippendale furniture is unlikely to want an article on racing pigeons or living in a squat, no matter how witty you are (unless the Marquis of Welshampton has suddenly taken up such activities, in which case you're OK).

The same rules apply for humourous articles as much as they do for any other kind. A common mistake for the beginner is to write a hilarious piece sending up a particular hobby or profession and to send it to a specialist magazine bought by people who pursue that particular hobby or profession. Train spotters do not need to be told that they are nerds. Lacemakers do not want to be informed that they are anal-retentives. A humour piece ridiculing teachers for their bad dress sense and untidiness is not going to sell to the *Times Educational Supplement* if all it seems to the editor is an attack on the profession. However, you can make a point if you disguise it well enough.

For instance, I once sold a humourous piece about the kinds of caravanners who drive badly to a caravanning magazine. Instead of taking the approach 'Aren't you fed up with all these caravanners who drive badly?', I made the point that not enough caravanners were driving badly and gave a full set of instructions on how do drive badly 'properly'. That way, those caravanners who think that inept caravan-towers give them all a bad name liked it because it reflected what they thought. The caravanners who did cause eight-mile tail-backs on a narrow lane in Cornwall will have missed the point, so they won't have been upset. In fact, people wrote into the magazine suggesting other strategies for driving badly.

So, if you still wanted to write your piece about teachers being scruffy and untidy, perhaps if you dressed it up as being a checklist for an OFSTED Inspector's report it might go down well, as it would poke more gentle fun at teachers at the same time as ridiculing the OFSTED report system.

Perhaps instead of thinking of humour as an entirely separate category, it is worth thinking of it as a means of enlivening your writing. Editors like touches of it in their articles. It doesn't have to be side-splitting; it doesn't even have to raise a smile. What it must do is stop what you are saying from being ordinary, bland and boring.

Inspirational

These often appear in the more downmarket women's magazines. You often see them with the strap line 'as told to ...' and are sometimes referred to as 'Triumph over Tragedy' articles. I am sure you know the kind of thing:

Betty Smith thought her world had fallen apart when she was diagnosed with gingivitis. However, Betty fought back and now not only has perfectly healthy gums, but has also set up a helpline for fellow sufferers. Betty tells the story of how she stared into the abyss of despair, but pulled herself back to live her life with renewed purpose, vigour and a fine pair of gums.

Perhaps that is a little unfair. Serious magazines and newspapers also carry these kinds of stories, even if the prose is a little less purple.

The difficulty is in finding these kinds of stories. Some journalists even advertise for people to come forward to share their true-life stories with a salacious readership. Personally I am not too keen on that – it smacks a little of exploitation. If you keep your eyes and ears open as you go about your daily life, you might come across a surprising number of people who have done startling and remarkable things, and who are genuinely an inspiration to others, without having to go ambulance-chasing.

Personal Experience

Of course, you may have a story of your own to tell. Many magazines love medical stories and if you have developed an unusual disease, you might find that you can write about it. However, you must ask yourself if you genuinely want your private life being placed in front of tens or even hundreds of thousands of readers.

If you have been a nurse, doctor, teacher, builder or had any particular set of skills at some point in your life, that experience can be put to good use for article writing. Although you may not be writing directly about your own experience, you will be putting that experience to use by using it to inform what you write. The astute article writer is going to view their personal experience as a springboard for all sorts of different ideas.

Nostalgia

As the population ages, so the market for nostalgia grows apace. However, almost everyone who retires and buys a word processor thinks that they can write about the past. One editor of a regional magazine tells me that he is inundated with nostalgic stories from older readers, who now live elsewhere in the country, about their schooldays in the region. He never publishes any of them.

It is a tough market and not necessarily a highly-paid one. A well-known national magazine that thrives on nostalgia pays less than £20 per thousand words. This would make you think that it would be an easy place for you to cut your teeth. After all, they are paying so little that they can't be getting many people writing for them. You would be surprised. I also have a suspicion that beginners see these magazines as easy targets. As a consequence, such magazines are inundated with dozens of pieces, most of which they are never going to use.

Do not assume that all the magazines aimed at the older age group are simply interested in nostalgia. Many magazines for mature readers see their readership as vibrant and forward-looking and have little room for nostalgia, so are simply unlikely to publish whimsical witterings. They want 'go-out-and-get-em' pieces for a readership that is not merely interested in knitting patterns, but in living a full and active life in retirement.

Service Pieces

You may occasionally hear the term 'service piece' bandied about in order to describe the kind of article where the writer looks at a range of vacuum cleaners/computers/wholemeal loaves and gives an explanation of the features and benefits of each one. Sometimes they do not even go so far as to make any real comparisons, but are simply a round-up of the latest gadgets that might be of use to their readers. Despite looking like work for the beginning writer these are nearly always done in-house.

Opinion Pieces

Many opinion pieces are clever, intelligent, witty and sharp, even if you don't agree with them. Then, when you look at some of the halfwits dragged in to write others, it is tough to stop your jaw from hitting your knees in disbelief. You may see semi-literate footballers who can scarcely manage to utter two syllables without the need to interject a swear word being given huge numbers of column inches. Or dim blondes from reality TV shows allowed to trill on for pages about the latest silly fashion accessory. If they are prepared to give such halfwits a chance to twitter on for a dozen paragraphs, they are bound to give space to an erudite, well-educated person like yourself whose every word, phrase and sentence oozes style ....

It would be a perfect world if only this were true. The reason Gary McThick and Hazel Twitterbrain get their columns is because they are famous for doing something else. For some reason, once you are famous, people want to know your opinion on everything. As for you, well I'm terribly sorry, but the editor doesn't know you from a bar of soap, so why on earth should they publish your views?

Besides, if all you want to do is express an opinion about something, why not write a letter? This isn't as stupid as it sounds as there are many newspapers and magazines that give away handsome prizes and even sizeable wodges of cash to letter writers as we have seen in Chapter 3.

If you can dress up your opinion in a humorous cloak, there may be a possible market for you. If not, just grit your teeth and read those pearls from Gary McThick.

Travel

Travel writing looks a doddle. You pack your anti-malaria tablets, a bottle of Scotch and a leather-bound notebook, then you go off to some wonderful paradise island where you knock out a thousand words and then spend the rest of the week in a series of blissful encounters with gorgeous members of the opposite sex – all at the magazine's expense. In fact, travel writing is one of the hardest sectors of the market to break into. There are hundreds of specialist travel writers out there and almost every freelance journalist has tried to earn an extra few bob by writing about their holiday in an article when they get back home.

One good way of starting is to use the area in which you live to find articles that will sell to national magazines. What may seem boring and everyday to you could be exciting and different to someone living elsewhere. Bear in mind that editors are often more likely to buy articles that give practical information than they are pieces that involve lots of description or personal opinions. Check out the magazine's mix and copy it.

Relationships

Women's magazines are bursting with stories about relationships. Most of them are aimed at either shedding light on the kind of relationship in which you are involved or titillating you with information about someone else's problems. Nonetheless, they constitute a large number of the articles that eventually do get published. If you have any kind of social work background or psychological training this could be fertile ground, but again, it is a crowded field.

The categories I have used here are not mutually exclusive, there is always going to be some kind of overlap. For instance, a funny article about your journey to pre-glasnost Kiev to take insulin to a group of diabetics could be seen as fitting into the categories of nostalgia, personal experience, humour, inspirational and travel. Nor is it a comprehensive list – I am sure that you can think of other possibilities, but these are some of the commonest types of article.

I am sure that you will find other possibilities as you read. Each time you come across an article and think 'I could have written that', try to come up with a similar idea that you could also write about.

Now that you have had a chance to think what you might write, let's have a look at how to write your article.

5 RESEARCHING YOUR ARTICLE

Most writers sell their ideas before writing the eventual article. However, as you have bought, borrowed or stolen this book, we will assume that you are new (or new-ish) to the writing game. If that is the case, then I recommend that you start by selling some finished articles so that you can build up a portfolio of work.

RESEARCHING YOUR IDEA

Once you have an idea for an article you will probably need to do some kind of research in order to be able to put some flesh on the bones. Research for article writing is not just a case of a quick glance in a general encyclopaedia. Nor is it (usually) as extensive and rigorous as one would expect academic research to be. For the purposes of writing articles, it is a good idea to consider research in two stages.

The first is a kind of 'scratch the surface' level, whereby you test your idea for an article to find out if you can get together enough background material to write it. If you decide that there is enough for an article, the second stage is to put together more in-depth information to flesh out your original idea. Even before you start researching, however, it is a good idea to think about how you are going to store the information once you have collected it.

Organizing Your Research Information

First and foremost, you need a filing system. Theoretically modern computers allow you to store huge amounts of information. If you do use a computer to store your records, don't forget to equip yourself with a means of backing it up. It would be awful if years of research were suddenly to disappear at the click of a mouse (or theft of your computer).

However, there is something so much more tactile about having paper-based information, so you should be realistic and recognize that you are probably going to need a proper filing cabinet or an equivalent. Home offices are now so common that a small filing cabinet can be picked up for around £35. If you are on a tight budget you can buy second-hand. You also do not necessarily have to buy the expensive suspension files to put in them.

Old A4 envelopes with the contents marked clearly on the front in felt-tip are a good way of storing information, at least to begin with. If you want to make life a little easier, you can make a list of what is in each drawer and stick it in the front. Box files are not a bad alternative.

A card index can be handy for keeping a few bullet-pointed notes of your own, but you are limited to the size of the cards. Always keep a stack of reporters' notebooks – they can be bought cheaply almost anywhere and they look the part. Treat your old notebooks as preciously as you would expenses receipts for the taxman. Store old ones for several years in a labelled shoebox. You never know when the information might come in handy again.

SOURCES OF RESEARCH INFORMATION

If you are going to write about your hobby or profession you are likely know where the best sources of information are to be found. Here we can only deal with research in a general way. What holds true for researching articles also applies to books, although books often involve more research, simply because they are larger undertakings.

Books

Before you even think of the wilder and more distant shores of research, do not forget the good old-fashioned book. If you have not done so already, it is worth beginning to build up your own library. I have listed a few books that I think are worth considering in the Appendix. As a minimum you need a dictionary, a thesaurus, a dictionary of quotations and a small encyclopaedia. Over the years you will build up a reference library that is tailored to the kind of writing you do.

If you are intending to specialize, it is worth developing your own small specialist library of books and magazines relevant to your field. Again, if you are going to be writing about your hobby or your profession, you may have the start of such a library already.

All of this book-buying can be hard on the purse, however. It is worth keeping an eye open in the charity shops and second-hand bookshops. Let your friends know that you are interested in a certain topic and you could be surprised at how generous they may be.

Libraries

Of course, owning books is great, but you can also borrow them. If you do not have a membership card for your local library, get one. As a writer, you need to give it your support by using it. After all, libraries are potential customers for when you write your book. Most librarians are highly-trained individuals and enjoy the challenge of helping one of their readers to find out information – it makes a change from taking in minor fines and re-stacking the shelves.

There are also specialist libraries. If you are a subject specialist you will probably know of any specialist libraries in your field. If you want to search through newspapers there are the national archive collections at British Library Newspapers in Colindale, North London and then there is the British Library itself, where many writers, including Karl Marx, have researched their books.

If you are writing local history it may be enough simply to visit the local history section of your branch library. However, if you need to go into a little more depth, you might have to try the nearest archives. They will almost certainly ask you to join; most are free or extremely cheap. If you do use local history resources, don't forget to take along a good supply of pencils, a rubber and a sharpener as most do not allow you to write in ink, in case you accidentally damage a manuscript.

You will probably have to learn how to use a microfiche reader, if you can't already. Many local newspapers are stored on microfiche; often these are linked to printers so you can print out the relevant section. If you find working in archives difficult, then it makes sense to be able to print out what you need and work on it at home. Increasingly it helps to be computer-literate or at least not to be daunted by equipment. However, do not fear, archivists are extraordinarily helpful wherever you go. Don't forget that without you there would be no archive service. In France, on one occasion, I had the entire archive staff fiddling with the apparatus so that I could get a printout of a document on microfiche.

The Internet

In reality the level of research needed for much non-fiction work can be conducted from the comfort of your own home. The explosion of resources on the Internet offers the writer vast research possibilities that would have demanded the services of a professional researcher only ten or fifteen years ago. It is also a godsend to people who live in remote areas.

The Internet is splendid for its vastness, but that is also its biggest drawback. You can find yourself with thousands of references to the subject you are investigating, much of which will be irrelevant. You have the added disadvantage that you cannot always be entirely sure about a website's accuracy. Still, if you learn to use the Web skilfully, it is the most fabulous toy a boy or girl could want.

Tips for Internet Research

- Use the advanced search features on your search engine – this helps to cut out unwanted references.
- If you use the Internet a lot, buy a subscription that gives unlimited access – broadband is worth every penny if you are a frequent user.
- Make sure your virus checker is bang up to date.
- Use a 'firewall' to protect your computer from being hacked into whilst you are online. There are several that are free to download.
- Be prepared to spend a lot of time trawling for information.

- If you pick up a piece of information that *has* to be accurate, try to double-check it against other sources. Information published on the Web is not always totally reliable.
- Don't be afraid to ask people you find on the Web to help you – it is amazing how generous they can be.
- Don't forget the Web is not just about the written word. You can download other things such as pictures or music as well.
- Earmark websites of use by putting them in your 'favourites' folder, you can always delete them at a later stage.
- Fill up your printer with used paper and put it into draft mode: this will save you a fortune on printout costs.
- If you use your credit card for Internet purchases, such as hard-to-find books, make sure that you are using a secure site.

Foreign Information

If you want information about foreign countries you could try their embassy or national travel information service. Many places have tourist information offices and these can also be useful. Again, the Internet is invaluable. We often pay for our holidays by writing travel pieces; before going we can order brochures of the area via the Web and work out possible articles beforehand.

If you are trying to access slightly more esoteric foreign information it is worth trying the Web before lashing out hundreds of pounds to go in person to check out one tiny fact. Similarly, if you know that you can get a piece of information from a particular source, sometimes simply writing or emailing will get what you want.

Interviews

One of the best ways for you to develop your own research is to conduct your own interviews. People are endlessly fascinating. We don't just want to read about the rich and famous, but ordinary people doing extraordinary things enthral us as well.

They do not just have to be face-to-face. You can conduct interviews over the telephone and even by post or email. It's a simple process, so long as you are well-prepared. If you are conducting a face-to-face interview then telephone, email or write to the person you are going to interview, setting out the details of the interview (date, time, venue, and so on) and letting them know how much time you will need – try to take as little as possible without skimping.

Dress appropriately. If you are meeting in an expensive restaurant with a dress code, then obey it; if you are going to be trudging through slurry on a cattle farm, wear wellingtons. When you arrive (punctually) for the interview, greet your interviewee politely. Do not simply launch into the interview straight away, but spend the first few minutes chatting and putting your interviewee (and yourself) at ease. If you are meeting in a bar or café, make sure you offer to buy a drink. However, don't fritter away the entire time devoted for the interview with idle chit-chat.

Before the interview itself, make sure that you have a list of questions. Make your questions 'open' rather than 'closed'. A closed question is one that can be answered with 'yes', 'no', or a simple fact. An open question allows the interviewee to give an opinion or to tell a story. For example, 'Am I right in saying that you recorded your first album in 2003?' is a bad question for two reasons. First, your interviewee can get away with a simple 'That's right.' Second, if your facts are wrong, it is not going to give the interviewee much faith in your background knowledge of his/her career. You will look like someone who simply hasn't done their homework.

'What was it like recording your first album?' is a better question. It may not be the best question ever devised, but you get the point. It gives the interviewee more scope. If he/she hesitates, you can ask 'Did you enjoy it?' or some other little prompting question to help get the ball rolling. Watch chat shows on television. Some chat shows are more about the host than they are about the guest. Look at the way in which some chat-show hosts ask questions. Some even answer their own questions, leaving the guest nowhere to go. See what works and copy it.

Don't stick rigidly to your pre-determined questions. If the interviewee veers off down an interesting path, then it can be fine to follow it. On the other hand, if you are trying to talk to a writer about her latest book, then an hour's worth of chat about her other books may be largely irrelevant, especially if you haven't got a huge number of words in which to write up the story.

If you are interviewing someone well known, then finding out some background about them isn't too hard – they may even have an agent or publicist who can let you have material. Do not be star-struck; treat everyone with the same politeness and friendliness with which you would like to be treated and you'll get on fine.

Use a tape recorder if appropriate. Always ask permission if you are going to record anyone or take their photo. If you are interviewing someone famous, they may bring along their own recording equipment, as they might have been misquoted in the past and want a record 'just in case'. Don't make a fuss about it; that's fine by you. You are professional enough not to misquote them anyway. If you want to record someone over the telephone, it is even more important to ask if it is all right to do so, as they can't see what you are doing. You can buy an inexpensive rubber suction microphone that you stick to the earpiece of the receiver. They aren't tremendous, as you will find a great deal of background noise, but are passable for occasional work. Buy something a little more upmarket if you are going to do a lot of telephone interviews.

At the end of the interview, thank your subject and give them some idea of when they are likely to see the piece if you know. Some interviewees ask to see the piece before publication. I am never entirely sure about this as, even if you have not said anything untoward, editors can chop and change things. On the other hand, on several occasions I have interviewed craftspeople working in fields about which I know nothing and run my piece past them to make sure that I've actually got it right. If you do show someone the piece you've written, then ask for immediate feedback, otherwise it simply adds another delay into the publishing process.

If you're not sure, then explain to the interviewee that you don't know the magazine's policy, but you will find out and let them know. Contact your editor, ask for their opinion and get back to the interviewee on the matter as soon as possible. Above all, don't make a fuss about it.

TO SUM UP

As you develop your own specialisms, you will begin to build up a picture of how and where to find your information. Just one final word of warning: research can be terribly addictive. You can get hooked on looking for information and end up writing very little. So, let's move on and start writing that article.

6 THE FUN BIT – WRITING YOUR ARTICLE

Now you have got your research information together, you need to start thinking about what to write. If you have already pitched your idea, you will have advanced some way along this stage and may be tempted to get straight down to the writing. If that suits your way of working – great, get on with it! But you may well find that a little while longer spent thinking about your subject will improve your article in the long run.

We have already seen how useful brainstorming and mind-mapping can be for developing ideas. You can also use it for the first step of the writing process or just use the more familiar linear notes. I am also a fan of 'marinating'. Simply mulling ideas over in your mind is a powerful way of getting to grips with a problem or coming up with a good sentence. Don't forget your notebook, though.

STRUCTURING YOUR ARTICLE

If you are a highly organized person who likes to know exactly what they are doing before they start writing, the next stage is to plan the structure of your article, so that it will have some kind of flow for the reader. On the other hand, if you find it difficult to impose a structure on your article before you start writing, you can always skip to the next stage – that of drafting – and impose some structure on it later. Whichever approach you choose, it is important to get your work into some kind of order at some stage. If you don't, you will end up with a series of disconnected ramblings.

In newspaper journalism, there is a tendency to organize articles on the basis of the importance of the various points in the article. Thus, the first sentence contains the most important information, with successive paragraphs containing information that the journalist sees as increasingly unimportant. This is because newspaper editors cut from the bottom.

With magazine feature articles, you don't have to limit yourself to this particular structure. Some articles, for instance, lend themselves to a chronological structure. If you are writing an article about someone who has suffered from a series of incidents of medical negligence, you might decide that this structure is best. You can play around with timescale in the same way that novelists and film-makers do: starting with a recent event, before going back to the point at which the story actually begins and then bringing it up to date. Alternatively, you might work your story towards a climax, starting with a series of minor but intriguing pieces of information until you leave the reader with your big show-stopping number in the final paragraph. Lists can also work reasonably well for the 'Seven Great Places to Eat in Scunthorpe' style of article. Not all of the article needs to be in a list form – you could top and tail the piece with an introduction and some kind of summary or conclusion.

Above all, when structuring your article, do not think of it as a school essay. Dull, worthy planning may look good pinned up on your notice-board before you start to write, but as soon as you have penned a few paragraphs you may find it acts more like a straitjacket than a plan.

DRAFTING

The next stage is commonly known as drafting; this is when you write your first version of the article, warts and all. Some people argue that they can't start anything until they have that first line of a piece firmly established. This is fine if you have the time, but most freelance writers simply have to get on with it. After all, you are writing an article that will be read at the dentist's, not a classic novel whose every word will be picked over by undergraduates for generations to come.

At this stage, you might find that simply jotting down a few sentences helps you to get going. If you keep a notebook, you may have some useful phrases noted down because one day you will find a use for them. Now is a good time to have a quick flick through and see if there is anything there that you could sensibly use. You may prefer using a tape recorder to dictate what you are going to write. However, no matter how long you put it off, there will come the time when you simply have to sit down and actually get something on paper or on your monitor.

One way to get the juices flowing is to use a technique that is known as 'free writing'. The concept of free writing is a straightforward one; it is based on the idea that there are two sides to the writer's personality. There is the creative self who can rattle out words by the yard, and the critical self who sits in judgement on what you have written.

To kick-start your writing it is best to forget your critical self for the time being and just get what you want to say down on paper. Do not worry about misspellings, bad grammar, appalling punctuation or false starts. Now is not the time for correcting your work (more of that later), now is the time simply to let what you have to say flood out. You can bring in your more critical alter ego later.

Once you have let your creative side have free rein, you should have the makings of an article. Of course your article is rough and ready, full of mistakes and even bursts of absolute gibberish. Don't worry about that. At least you have now got the raw materials from which you can sculpt the finished piece. It does not matter how much you change your original draft as long as you provide the editor with the kind of article that you promised in the first place, or if you are submitting on spec, an article that is appropriate.

Titles

You should already have a working title. You may also find that it is the one thing about your articles that does get altered by an editor – don't be miffed if this happens. If you loved your own title that dearly, keep it for another article.

If you have come up with what you think is a great title, but have no idea when to use it, then keep a note of it in your notebook and use it for another piece at a later stage. In fact, if you ever come up with a little phrase that you think might make a good title, be sure to note it down. A good title is hard to come by.

If you strain to be too clever in your titling, it may be as well to think of three general categories from which to take your title. There are of course as many types of title as there are titles themselves, but at least this method works reasonably well.

Simple Declarative Statement. A useful, but frequently overlooked way of starting an article is by telling the reader exactly what to expect. An article entitled 'How to feed a scout group for under a fiver' tells you precisely what the article is going to be about. It may not be the cleverest title in the magazine, but at least you know what you are getting.

Question. The question is often used to provoke some kind of response. 'So you think you know all there is to know about acne?' is the form often used in women's magazines. You must then make sure your article actually answers the question.

Quotation or Saying. An apt quotation or saying can be a useful way of starting a piece – 'A woman is a woman, but a good cigar is a smoke', but if the quotation is especially well known, it may be worth giving it a bit of a twist – 'The email of the species is more deadly than the mail', which is in itself close enough to the idea of the pun. An article about fishing might be called 'Hooked on Salmon', for instance.

Opening Paragraph

The trick with any form of writing is to get the reader to read the next bit. If the title of your article catches the reader's eye, he or she will probably read the first paragraph. You then need a good opening line to keep the reader's attention through the first paragraph and then make him or her carry on until the end of your piece. If you look through a magazine you will come across a variety of openings. Often they use the same kinds of techniques as for titles.

Sometimes, giving the reader a shock works well. 'By the time you finish reading this sentence, three children will have been eaten by crocodiles' is enough to get most people reading further. In this particular case, it also has the benefit of incorporating a bizarre statistic, which is another strong way to start a story.

A declarative statement, telling the readers what the story is about has the advantage of being simple and straightforward. 'Albert Smith has been digging his allotment for forty-eight years' tells us the name of the person the article is about and something of his background. Alternatively, a question ('Who actually did kill Cock Robin?') intrigues the reader.

Bizarre Facts and Figures

You would probably be amazed at the way in which the odd or esoteric grabs readers' imaginations. Did you know, for instance, that 60,000 people in the UK are taken to hospital each year because of packaging-related accidents? Or, that the French–Algerian writer Albert Camus is the only man to have played in the football World Cup finals and to have won the Nobel Prize for Literature? No? I've been saving those facts for years in the hope that they might come in handy one day and, sure enough, they just have. People like odd and obscure information; it also somehow seems to get the reader onto your side.

Subheadings

It's rare to find an article that isn't subdivided in some way. Most articles need breaking up into digestible parts – sort of mini-chapters within a piece. One way of doing this is to use subheadings, which are in effect titles within the article. Give some thought to these subheadings as they also act as little hooks to draw the reader further into the article. They are also a useful way of planning an article as they can help you to cluster your ideas around a particular theme or concept. However, not all magazines use subheadings. Check the house style of the publication you are aiming at and keep to it.

Sidebars

Sidebars are the little boxes alongside the text. They often contain bullet-pointed information, contact addresses or other sorts of information in brief. If you have information that sits uneasily in the main body of the article or slows down the pace, then move it to a sidebar. This book, for instance, has various little boxes and lists – these are sidebars.

A MATTER OF STYLE

All this makes article writing sound like a mechanistic and technical process. This is true to an extent; writing is both an art and a craft. So, let us turn our attention to some of those elements of writing that make what we write enjoyable for the reader. I am going to group these together under the heading of 'style', although I suspect that, strictly speaking, they amount to more than that.

It is hard to define the word 'style'. Some articles that you read have a 'sense of style' that others lack. This is the idea of style in its grandest form: elegant, sweeping sentences; words chosen with immaculate care. Sure, you can develop this kind of style over the years and, if you are lucky and talented, you may have it from the outset. For the rest of us, we plod on, hoping that the next sentence will be better tuned than the last.

For our purposes here, it is probably more useful to think of style in less grandiose terms. If you think of style as simply being an approach to your writing, there are certain strategies that you can use to make your writing better and more readable. For instance, I hope that the style of this book is accessible, informal – chatty, even. My aim is that the book should give the impression that we are having a conversation, not as though you are wading your way through a treacly textbook. I have no pretensions that the book has 'style', however. On the other hand, if you were writing a biography you would probably use a slightly more formal style, although you would still need to avoid being grandiose.

Your main aim as a non-fiction writer is to convey information to your readers. This is as true of a straightforward how-to book as it is of a narrative history. If you write anything that baffles or bamboozles, you will lose your readers. Yet, at the same time, you want what you write to be entertaining. If you reduce language to the level of an instruction leaflet for flat-pack furniture, it hardly grabs the reader. Most of the time, you want to be aiming for a relaxed, conversational style that draws in the reader. Some non-fiction is, of course, more literary than this. But for the most part, non-fiction writing needs to be clear, concise and precise.

One of the masters of straightforward English was George Orwell. He is best known nowadays as a novelist, but was also a journalist and essayist who was passionate about writing in clear English. In 1946, he wrote a classic essay entitled *Politics and the English Language*, in which he castigates sloppy writing, trotting out wonderful examples of bad prose that he calls a 'catalogue of swindles and perversions'. His main target was political writing but what he suggests is applicable to non-fiction writing in general. As a means of combating the writing of 'swindles and perversions' Orwell suggests a series of six rules, which we will look at in turn. The rules are Orwell's, the comments mine:

Never Use a Metaphor, Simile or Other Figure of Speech That You are Used to Seeing in Print

A cliché is a phrase or saying that has become tired and frazzled from overuse, such as *raining cats and dogs*, *as bold as brass*, or *happy as Larry*. As one wag put it – you should avoid clichés like the plague. The reason these phrases are popular is that, to begin with, they conjure up a new image. Alas, with repeated use, they conjure up no image at all and are simply lazy writing. If you find that you have written a cliché, replace it with something sharper.

Never Use a Long Word Where a Short One Will Do

You need to remember that you are writing for clarity and not to show off. Sometimes we fall into the trap of being too 'writerly', which we do when we are trying too hard. Take a step back from your work, read it out aloud, and relax into a more conversational mode. It's important for you to write the best English you possibly can; the best English is not always the cleverest English. Calling a horse an 'equine quadruped' is convoluted. You may have an impressive vocabulary, but now is the time to wear that learning lightly. Sending readers scurrying to the dictionary every other paragraph is not going to endear you to them.

You were probably taught at school that repeating the same word in an essay is an example of bad style. There is some truth in this. Unfortunately, if you are writing an article on gladioli, for instance, there is a limit to the number of different words you can use to replace 'gladioli'. If you want, you can use a thesaurus to liven up your writing by finding alternatives to any words that you seem to be overusing. But there are dangers: there is little worse than reading a report of a football match and discovering the kind of language that gives us 'Smith slid the orb beyond the reach of the man in the green jersey'. Use words that are right for the context.

If it is Possible to Cut a Word Out, Always Cut it Out

This is where many of us stumble. It is especially true if you are attempting to write in an informal style. There are many phrases that slip into our writing, almost without our realizing; I'm sure there are examples in this book. In general, use a word rather than a phrase wherever possible. For example:

Long	Short
in order to	to
at this point in time	now
with the result that	so/thus
a great deal of	most
in the event of	if
as a matter of fact	in fact

Also look out for 'intensifiers'. These are words such as *quite, very, pretty, totally, extremely* that creep into phrases such as 'the place was pretty creepy'. Well, was it creepy or wasn't it?

Too many adjectives (describing words) in your writing can also be off-putting. It is actually easy, simple, straightforward and undemanding to write lists of adjectives. Choose just one telling adjective or phrase. I recently read a piece in which a large rock was described as looking like an Easter Island statue. That tells me everything I need: telling me that it is towering, craggy, lofty, impressive, almost human, weathered and so on doesn't actually add anything that I can't conjure up from the 'Easter Island' reference.

Adverbs (words that add to the verb and often end in -ly) tend to make writing flabby and are often the preserve of purple-ish romantic fiction. Whenever you find yourself qualifying a verb with an adverb, see if you can come up with a stronger verb. So, for instance, if you are writing about a man walking slowly down the road, we know far more about him if he is shambling or limping or hobbling or sloping or ambling or tottering or swaying than we do if he is just 'walking slowly'.

Orwell's Rules for Writing Clear English

- Never use a metaphor, simile or other figure of speech that you are used to seeing in print.
- Never use a long word where a short one will do.
- If it is possible to cut a word out, always cut it out.
- Never use the passive where you can use the active.
- Never use a foreign phrase, a scientific word or a jargon word if you can think of an everyday English equivalent.
- Break any of these rules sooner than say anything outright barbarous.

Never Use the Passive Where You Can Use the Active

If you write 'the man was bitten by the dog', the sentence you have written is in the passive voice. 'The dog bit the man' is active voice. The advantage of the active voice over the passive is that it is much more immediate. It draws in the reader, turning what you are writing into something that seems nearer to fiction-writing than the world of the management report.

Never Use a Foreign Phrase, a Scientific Word or a Jargon Word if You Can Think of an Everyday English Equivalent

Orwell was even opposed to phrases such as *cul-de-sac* and *status quo*, although these have passed into the language. I suspect that authors using foreign phrases may be showing off their linguistic skills and knowledge. Perhaps they think that it adds a *je ne sais quoi* to their work. They are falling into the trap of setting out to impress, whereas they should be aiming for clarity.

Break Any of These Rules Sooner than Say Anything Outright Barbarous

There's an old saying that 'rules are for the obedience of fools and the guidance of wise men'. This is Orwell's get-out-of-gaol clause. If you live in a *cul-de-sac*, then it is perfectly all right to describe it as such. What are you going to call a *baguette*? A French stick? But, if we're being incredibly literal, a French stick is a *bâton*, which in English is used to conduct an orchestra. And even if we do come up with some description, the French have all sorts of long, thin loaves, such as the *ficelle*, the *bâtard*, the *flûte* and the *pain* itself. Besides, more importantly, we know what a *baguette* is nowadays.

Similarly, writers often use overblown language for comic effect. You could substitute the sentence 'I was lying' for 'I was being economical with the truth,' but 'there is a certain subtlety of meaning that disappears with this.

Even if you don't fully agree with everything that Orwell says on style, you must surely see the thrust of his argument.

Once you have looked at your work from a stylistic point of view, it is worth bearing in mind the following points:

Sentence and Paragraph Length

It is important to get your average sentence length correct. A tabloid newspaper is going to want shorter, pithier sentences than a more discursive article in a serious broadsheet. If you know your target market, work out the average sentence length of the kind of article you are writing and stick to it. Roughly fifteen words per sentence is a good target if you're not sure.

If you calculate that the average sentence length is fifteen words, then that does not mean that every sentence you write has to be fifteen words long. Uniform sentence lengths make tedious reading. Shorter sentences speed up the text. To slow the reader down, use longer, more languorous sentences, which may take a little more time to make their point, but which will have the effect of lulling the reader along. It's simple.

Paragraphs should be short. If you find that a paragraph runs on for a dozen or more lines, try to split it up. The white space created by gaps between paragraphs, or the indentation at the beginning, actually helps the eye to focus and makes your work easier to read.

Linking

When you read through your work, it should move seamlessly from one paragraph to the next as far as possible. To make sure that your prose doesn't 'clunk', you need to check to make sure that one idea follows on from the next and that you have used some kind of appropriate phrase to join the two ideas, sentences, or paragraphs.

Anecdotes

Little personalized stories often go down well with readers: they can add a touch of humanity to more serious articles and are the mainstay of populist magazines. Be careful when using anecdotes from your own life though, especially if they involve other people. A writer must decide exactly how much of him or herself to project into a story. Only use anecdotes when they are relevant and they are either amusing or the reader can learn from them.

Quotations

The odd quotation is not just useful for titles and openers, but livens up a text. You can either use quotations that have been gathered in anthologies or special collections, or you can quote people who have contributed to the research you needed to undertake to write your article. When quoting your interviewees be as accurate as possible, although it is only polite to leave out all their 'ers' and 'ums'; we all do it and you don't want to make them sound like idiots.

Description and Narrative

Description can be a powerful tool. Travel writing, for instance, often demands it. As far as possible, though, you should try to work your description seamlessly into the story you are trying to tell. If you are writing up an interview

Using the Five Senses to Create a Scene

Autumn has come to this part of Switzerland. The days are shorter and
cool more quickly as the sun sets behind the hills.
*   The last of the cattle have clanked their way down the hillside for milking*
and Madame Richard is testing the casserole which has been simmering
on the stove for most of the day. As she lifts the lid, the aroma of red wine
and onions fills the little kitchen.

If we don't quite use all five senses here, we certainly hint at them. Sight (the
hills), sound (clanking) and smell (red wine and onions) are directly covered.
Taste is implied from the casserole and the idea that the days are cooler could
possibly be described as touch. Even in a deliberately simple example like this,
you can see how easy it is to bring a scene to life using this straightforward
technique.

Exercise: Description – Using the Five Senses

Think about a place you have visited. It doesn't necessarily have to be overseas,
it could be somewhere nearer home. It could be bustling or peaceful, exciting or
dull. Conjure up a picture of that place in your mind. Take your notepad and jot
down some words that occur to you as you hold that image in your thoughts.
Make sure that you have words that appeal to each of the senses:

sight   sound   taste   touch   smell

After a few minutes' note-taking, write a piece of around 300 words to
describe the scene. You will find that as you do this, you will bring in the sixth
sense – atmosphere.

intersperse your interviewee's speech with a couple of lines of description or
comment from time to time. It breaks up the text and makes it easier to read.

It is also useful to think in terms of the five senses when writing description.
If you can appeal to all five senses then you are going to broaden your appeal
amongst the readership: some readers are attracted to taste, others sight,
sound, touch or smell. Capture these in your writing and you will be adding a
further dimension to your work.

EDITING YOUR OWN WORK

Hopefully you will soon be using many of these techniques, even when you are
writing at full speed and are more concerned with getting words on the page
than with the prose style. However, whatever you write will always need editing. Don't regard editing as a chore; see it as the way in which you are going
to use a touch of the alchemist's art. You are now going to change the base
metal of your frantic scribblings into gold.

Once you have finished an article, put it to one side for a while – it is impossible to check something you have only just written. The playwright Joe Orton used to put his plays away in a drawer for three months before re-reading them. Try to leave your work alone for at least a week.

Meaning
The first thing to do is to read through your rough draft to see if it makes sense. Re-work anything that doesn't, even if it is not precisely what you had in mind stylistically.

Energy
No matter what publication you are writing for, your article needs energy. However, you must bear in mind the audience for whom you are writing and ensure that your style of writing is going to appeal to that particular audience. Cut anything that slows the pace of your piece unless it is done for deliberate effect.

Accuracy of Facts
You need to check your facts rigorously to ensure that everything in your article is accurate. You also need to bear in mind how many facts your audience wants and how much explanation they need. An article for a British climbing magazine, for instance, will insult its readership if it tells them that Scafell is in the Lake District. On the other hand a magazine for overseas visitors on coach tours will expect you to cast light on that kind of matter.

Final Edit
As a final read-through before looking for minor mistakes, ask yourself some questions:

- Can you improve on any turns of phrase?
- Is there anything that sounds clumsy?
- Have you used a particular word too often?
- Are you conveying the right 'tone of voice'?
- Are you being patronizing or too chummy?
- Are you talking directly to your readership? Or does what you have written sound like the instructions for a flat-pack wardrobe?

Proofreading
Before you lay out your work in the way in which the editor wants it, you need to do that last thorough check for spelling, grammar and punctuation. It is always useful if you can enlist the help of somebody else at this stage to give the manuscript a last once-over to check for any details that have gone astray.

There's no need for you to use any of the traditional proofreader's marks, as you are only doing it for yourself. In fact, it is only worth learning the marks if you are frequently given your drafts back to check – something that happens infrequently in the magazine world, but which is more usual with a book.

Congratulations! Your article is now finished, all you need to do now is to lay it out in an acceptable format and you are ready to approach editors.

P.S. Don't forget that, although this chapter is called 'Writing Your Article', almost everything that has been said here is equally applicable to writing a book.

Exercise: Writing an Article

By now you should have enough material to write an article. Choose a magazine that you think you could write for and pick a topic to write on. Do not worry at this stage about whether you are likely to sell the article or not. This is an exercise; if you do come up with something saleable, regard it as a bonus. Make sure that your article fits the kinds of subjects, article length and style of your target magazine.

When you have finished the article, put it away for at least a week before looking at it and putting into practice the editorial advice in this chapter. When you've done that, ask yourself if you honestly believe that this piece is the kind of thing that the magazine would buy. If it is, send it off.

---

7 SELLING YOUR ARTICLE

The usual way to sell an article is by selling it in proposal form, known as a 'pitch'. You can do this by phoning, emailing or writing to the editor of your target publication. However, I think it is rather difficult to pitch ideas if you don't have a track record or haven't got a professional reputation in a particular field. If you are a barrister who has just defended a high-profile murder case and whose client was controversially given a 'not guilty' verdict, then no one will care about your actual writing experience. For the rest of us, being able to show that we can do the work is vital.

> You ring the editor and say 'I've got an article on bunions in guinea pigs.'
> 'Great,' says the editor. 'Who else have you written for?'
> 'Err ... err ... err.'

If you've got lots of chutzpah, you might get away with it. Most of us couldn't. This is why it is probably worth sending out a few completed articles speculatively, just to see if anyone will bite.

To do this, put your finished article into the format described later in this chapter, together with a covering letter (*see* example on page 52) and a stamped, self-addressed envelope (SAE). Send a finished article to one editor at a time. If you haven't heard anything after about six to eight weeks, then you can follow this up with a polite enquiry letter or phone call. If they then haven't had the decency to reply – you'd think they would have a standard rejection letter that they can print out and stick in an SAE – then try elsewhere.

Don't just send out one article; try to get several circulating. Statistically, regardless of how good your articles are, you stand a better chance of acceptance with more of them in circulation.

Sample Covering Letter to an Editor Enclosing an Article

Deirdre Barrowclough
1, The Avenue, Scuttleborough, Lincolnshire, ZF23 2RT
Tel/Fax 01000 – 9876 543   Email: fb@scuttleborough.com

Ms Helen Smith
Editor, Guinea Pigs Galore Magazine
Rest of the address and postcode   Date

Dear Ms Smith,

Solving Your Guinea Pig's Bunion Problem

Many guinea pigs suffer from bunions, yet this is a problem that can be easily treated.

I have been a guinea pig chiropodist for several years and have developed several strategies for dealing with foot problems in cavies.

Please find enclosed an article of 1,000 words entitled 'Treating Bunions in Guinea Pigs', based on my experience, which I hope will be suitable for your 'Minor Ailments' section.

I also enclose a disk on which you will find a series of good-quality digital pictures showing the bunion-treating process as well as a computer file of the article saved in both Word and Text formats and a stamped, addressed envelope for your convenience.

Yours sincerely,

Deirdre Barrowclough

SELLING A PROPOSAL

Let's hope that within a few months you are beginning to have some success. Some articles will come bouncing back, others will get lost in the ether, a few might be taken up by editors.

Once you have begun to sell some articles, then you are in a good position to start pitching ideas. When you get to this stage, you will see that pitches have several advantages over writing complete pieces and sending them out speculatively. You don't have to write the whole article. If it normally takes you a whole day to write an article, but just an hour to write a decent pitch, then you are managing your time far better by writing the pitch.

Articles are rejected for many reasons. More often than not, they are turned down simply because that subject has recently been covered or is just about to be covered. By sending a pitch, you are cutting down on your work. I have been trying to sell an article about Zeppelins for ages now. Nobody seems to want to buy it. If I had written the article, I'd have wasted a lot more time than

I have simply sending out the germ of an idea. Similarly, a magazine that often takes travel pieces from me wasn't interested in a recent idea, because they had already accepted a piece on that area.

Professional writers sell their articles by approaching magazines with ideas. If you want to be viewed as a professional, this is the approach to take. Writing the pitch often tells you whether or not your idea could make an article. As you prepare to explain to the editor what approach you are taking, you will sometimes find that what seemed like a good idea doesn't actually stand up after all.

You can also pitch to more than one magazine at a time; you can't do that with the finished item. It is not an approach that I would heartily endorse as it can lead to problems. However, I occasionally pitch the same idea simultaneously to magazines in the UK and in the States, as they are buying different publication rights.

If you make simultaneous pitches in the UK, you have to be careful. You need an article that can be tailored to suit different magazines, then if more than one editor accepts your idea, you can write your piece for that market. If your piece can't easily be altered however, then stick with approaching one magazine at a time.

The Pitch – Writing a Query Letter

Think of a query letter as being your main sales tool. Your aim is to sell your article to the editor. Imagine you are the editor: what do you want? Most editors probably want a good idea with an interesting angle to it. They want to know that you are capable of writing this article well, both in terms of your writing ability and knowledge of the subject. They want to know when they can have the article and that when they do get it, they will not have to do a lot of work to it to make it fit the magazine.

Your query letter is where you have to demonstrate all this to an editor. One approach that works well is to make sure you consider the following points in your pitch (*see* example on page 57).

Names and Forms of Address
Get the editor's name and write to them using it. If you are using a press guide or a yearbook, always telephone the magazine switchboard just to check on the name of the editor. If the editor is a woman, ensure that you know whether she likes being addressed as Miss, Mrs or Ms. Do not address the editor by his or her first name until you have developed some kind of relationship with them. If writing 'Dear Mr (or Ms/Mrs) Smith ...' sign off with 'yours sincerely' and not 'yours faithfully'.

Letters addressed 'Dear Sir or Madam' indicate that you don't know enough about the magazine. 'Dear Bob', when you don't even know Bob, is far too matey (especially as he prefers to be called Robert anyway).

Title of the Article

Always try to think of a title for your article, even if it is only a working title. It is a good way of focusing on the central idea for your piece – it will also help to convey that to an editor.

Sample Paragraph

Including an example of a pertinent paragraph is a useful little trick. Normally this would be the first paragraph. It shows the editor that you can write well and in a style that will draw in the readership of their particular magazine.

The Angle of the Article

It is not enough simply to have an idea for an article – it needs to be developed and refined so that you have an angle of focus for what you want to write about. Write this section of your letter from the point of view of the reader, letting the editor know exactly what the reader will gain from your article. Use phrases such as 'I will show the reader ...' to convey to the editor just how reader-friendly you are.

Identifying a particular section of the magazine that you think would be a good spot for your article is also a useful trick. It shows that you are familiar with the magazine and have thought about your contribution in relation to it. Drop in a clue that shows you know the magazine. For instance, using a semi-technical term like 'sidebar' gives the impression that you know some of the jargon of the trade.

Why You are the Person to Write It

The editor probably has people queuing up to pitch ideas for stories. You need to persuade the editor that you are in a good position to write this article. You need to be able to show that you are qualified to write on the topic (whether by formal qualification, expertise or knowledge).

If you have some relevant, recent clips (photocopies of published articles), enclose them. I do mean relevant: if you have written one of those confessional features for a weekly women's magazine ten years ago, then it is probably not going to be very useful to show to the editor of a fishing magazine. Ensuring that the editor knows that your information is up to date is also a good ploy. You can now see how getting a few articles published by sending them out speculatively can help you to get further work.

Additional Information

Let the editor know when the article is going to be available and if there is any other support material that will be of use. The most common type of support material is likely to be pictures, but could also include maps, drawings, paintings, diagrams, archive material – in fact anything that isn't continuous text.

Working on the basis that you don't want to offend an editor, it is also best to enclose an SAE, or if pitching to an editor abroad include with it an International Reply Coupon. (You can buy IRCs at your local post office and they can be exchanged abroad for the value of a return stamp.)

Final Check
The query letter is your calling card. It is so easy to misspell things, omit a word or, in the modern world of the computer spellchecker, to have silly mistakes such as 'their' for 'there' or 'to' for 'too' pass you by. Get someone else to proofread your letter. As with all forms of writing, if you can leave the completed work aside for a week then checking it will become much easier. If you don't have anyone to help you then read it back to yourself, sentence-by-sentence, in reverse order.

Make sure that your typing is tidy and that you have printed your letter on one side of the paper only and preferably only used a single sheet of paper for the job. If you are using a computer, then you should not have to make any corrections in pen on your letter. Also, if you have said in your letter that you have enclosed an SAE, check to make sure that it is there.

SOME IMPORTANT DO-NOTS

Do Not Tell an Editor that You are New to the Game
'But everyone has to start somewhere,' I hear you cry. True, and editors know this. But why should they trust a complete novice to write an article when they know dozens of old hands they can rely on? You may be twice as good as these old hacks, but it's irrelevant. The old hacks have proved over the years that they can produce what the editor wants time and time again. They are known and reliable.

Do Not Ask for Contributors' Guidelines in a Query Letter
This is a silly mistake to make; you want the editor to think that you know the magazine inside out. You should have got your contributors' guidelines weeks ago. Your letter is now giving out a mixed message. It's saying 'Here's a great idea for an article, oh and by the way, do you publish this sort of thing?'

Do Not Set Yourself a Deadline You Can't Meet
Unless an idea is time-dependent – based on an anniversary or something topical – it probably does not matter if it is published today or in six months' time. If you tell an editor that you can get an article to him/her within a week but it takes you two weeks, it looks much worse than giving a four-week deadline and delivering in just three weeks; it's basic psychology.

Do Not Make Your Letter Too Long
An editor wants to know that you can get your ideas across succinctly. If you can't explain in one page why you should be writing this particular

article for this particular magazine, how are you going to write a great, tight article for the magazine? One page is best. If you are submitting a batch of ideas, then I think it is best to write a covering letter and then enclose the ideas as a separate document. Use plenty of 'white space' in your letters and queries in order to make them easier to read and therefore more appealing.

Do Not Admit Previous Disappointments
Confessing that this is the nineteenth time you have submitted this idea to a magazine means that the editor is going to think that you are a failure. Literary agents may relish the time that they picked up a best-selling author who had already been turned down by everyone else in the business, but the average editor of a mainstream magazine is unlikely to be looking to unearth the latest literary talent. Editors want something much more mundane than that; they want someone who can deliver exactly what they want, when they want it. If three other editors have turned down your idea, then telling Editor No. 4 isn't going to help your cause.

Do Not Moan About a Rival Publication
These editors often know each other. There may be commercial rivalry between two magazines publishing along similar lines, but the editors could well be mates. It does you no favours to criticize the opposition. Besides, you might want to write for the opposition one day yourself.

Do Not Pester an Editor
Some magazines are appallingly slow in responding to ideas, some are prompt indeed. It is not unusual for a magazine to take months before it comes back to you with a reply. Editors have holidays, sick leave and maternity leave, and are often extremely busy. Allow six to eight weeks before chasing up a query.

Do Not Admit that You Have Never Read
the Magazine
There is no need to pretend that you are the magazine's number-one fan, but telling the editor you have never read the magazine is foolish. They want to know that you can fit in with the house style and have an understanding of what the readers want. A positive comment about a recent article in your query letter is useful, but don't over-egg the pudding. Editors don't want to hear from sycophants.

Do Not Tell the Editor His or Her Job
Never write 'Your magazine would be much better if ...'. Editors need to be supplied with positive ideas, not given a thorough knocking over the things they're not doing to your satisfaction.

Sample Letter to an Editor Pitching an Idea

Deirdre Barrowclough
1, The Avenue, Scuttleborough, Lincolnshire, ZF23 2RT
Tel/Fax 01000 – 9876 543 Email: fb@scuttleborough.com

Ms Helen Smith
Editor, Guinea Pigs Galore Magazine
Rest of the address and postcode   Date

Dear Ms Smith,

Solving Your Guinea Pig's Bunion Problem

Goldie the guinea pig can hardly walk. When she does, it is obvious that she is in pain. She doesn't like anyone touching her paws. If they do, she recoils. On some days, the pain is so bad, she even refuses food.

Goldie may well be suffering from bunions. This is a common disease amongst guinea pigs and one that can be cured successfully by the guinea pig owner without running up huge vet's bills.

In an article of 1,000 words, I would show your readers how to prevent such problems occurring and how to deal with them when they do.

I have been a guinea pig chiropodist for several years and have developed several strategies for dealing with foot problems in cavies.

I enclose a stamped, addressed envelope for your convenience, but am equally happy to be contacted by phone or via email.

I look forward to hearing from you.

Yours sincerely,

Deirdre Barrowclough

THE EDITOR'S REPLY

Aha, through your door comes an envelope you recognize. It is a self-addressed envelope, obviously a reply from one of your attempts to sell an article. With trembling, marmalade-sticky fingers, you rip open the envelope and read the reply. What will the editor have said?

'No.'

Or, if you're lucky, 'no thank you'. This is not especially helpful: you don't know why they don't want your piece. However, it is not the editor's job to pass opinion on your work, they just decide whether to use it or not. Bad luck.

'No thank you, because ...'.

This is a little more useful. You are unlikely to be told that your article isn't accepted because it's not good enough, but you may get some other useful information. An explanatory note that indicates that a magazine covered this subject recently, has a similar subject in the pipeline or has a policy of not including articles on this subject (I have encountered a 'no alcohol' policy on two occasions) is helpful. Occasionally, an editor might even suggest that you try another publication.

If you get any praise at all, then think of it as a near miss. And if the editor says any of the following:

'No, but if you change ... I'll publish it.'

Change whatever it is and send it back. Promptly.

'I'll keep it for publication at some future date.'

A bit naughty. They should give you a date, but at this stage, be happy. It's a result – of sorts.

'I would like to see the finished article before deciding.'

If you have started to pitch articles then you might get this kind of reply. It's a bit half-hearted, but at least there is a glimmer of hope. Write the article to the best of your ability and send it off. Don't be too dejected if the finished article is then rejected, you have probably encountered a real belt-and-braces editor, who has difficulty making decisions. Send the finished piece off elsewhere if they do the dirty on you.

'Yes, we'd like to publish it in our October issue.'

Bingo. Ask if they pay now or upon publication.

PRESENTING YOUR WORK TO EDITORS

When an article is accepted for publication, you need to lay it out in a way that is acceptable to an editor. This also applies to articles written on spec. Some of the rules for doing this are rather quaint and date from the time when type-setting was done by hand. There is often no logic for why it should still be done like this, save that it is a tradition. It also proves to an editor that you are a professional writer.

Ideally, you should use a computer or word processor (*see* Chapter 12). If you do not have either of these, then a typewriter will do, but be sparing in your use of correction fluid. A messy manuscript looks unprofessional and could be one of the reasons you get rejected. Never submit a handwritten article; no one is ever going to look at it. Also, don't forget to clip your manuscript together using a paper clip. For some reason pins and staples are not popular amongst editors.

Page Layout
There are several ways of laying out the page, but here is one that seems to be acceptable to editors:

- Use plain, white A4 paper and print or type on one side only.
- Make sure that your work is double-spaced. Set your margins to approximately 3.5cm (1½in 'in old money'). The first paragraph of each section should be blocked to the margin.
- Indent the first line of the second and subsequent paragraphs. Do not insert a double-space between paragraphs. Do not right-justify your work (align the right-hand side of the page) – just leave it jagged down the right-hand edge. And no, I don't know why. Suffice it to say that editors don't like it, so don't do it.
- Do not try to be too stingy when it comes to using paper. Use a font size of either eleven or twelve, never anything smaller. Your finished work must look easy to read. If you have a choice of fonts and font sizes, use a standard one rather than anything too fancy.
- Do not change typefaces within an article unless there is a good reason for it – for example, if you are writing an article about typefaces and want to illustrate Courier and Times New Roman. Use a good, clear typeface.
- Use the left-hand footer to include a version of the title and the right-hand footer for the page number. It is useful to use the numbering system 'page x of y', so that the editor knows exactly how many pages they should have and at the end of an article, after all the sidebars, type the word 'ends'. Newspaper journalists use a slightly different method.
- Use the word-counting facility on your computer to work out how many words you have written, or if you are steam-driven, do an average-line count. I tend to round up the number of words to the nearest fifty until 1,000, then I work to the nearest 100, but this is not a hard-and-fast rule. Never, ever give an exact word count – '567 words' – for some reason this is a sure-fire giveaway that you are an amateur. Remember, you want to seem like a professional at all times.
- Always supply your work on disk, saved as a text file as well as whatever word-processing program you use (such as Microsoft Word) as magazines often use Apple Macs and you are saving the magazine a retyping job. Don't forget to label the disk clearly with your name, the title of the article, the file name you have used and the format in which you have saved it.

Cover Sheet
Some people reckon the cover sheet is the sign of an amateur. It might be, but I am reliably informed that its use is widespread. If you are using a cover sheet (don't bother with one if you are sending your article via email), keep it simple.

In the middle of the page give the title of the article and your name. In one of the corners, perhaps in a smaller typeface, re-state your name and give your address, telephone and fax numbers and email address, if appropriate. In another corner, state your word count and write 'Copyright Fred Bloggs', or use the © sign if you can find it on your computer, and add the words 'FBSR offered' if it is for a British publication.

FBSR stands for First British Serial Rights. It is a bit of legal jargon that means that you are giving this magazine the chance to publish this article first and that no one else has published it already in the UK. (*See* the example cover sheet below). If you are selling to the USA or Canada, use the abbreviation FNASR – First North American Serial Rights.

Feature
1,700 words
FBSR offered

Deirdre Barrowclough
1, The Avenue,
Scuttleborough,
Lincolnshire,
ZF23 2RT
Tel/Fax 01000 – 9876 543
Email: fb@scuttleborough.com

Solving Your Guinea-Pig's Bunion Problem

Deirdre Barrowclough

© Deirdre Barrowclough

---

8 Writing a Book Proposal

If you start to sell your articles and are beginning to feel that you are having some success as a writer, you might want to try writing a complete book. Of course, there is no reason why you shouldn't simply skip the article-writing stage and go straight for the book. However, a book is an ambitious project if you don't know for certain that you can write to a publishable standard. Also, if you do have a track record of published work, it will make it easier to sell your book.

If you were a new novelist, you might, with enormous good fortune, sell your book on the strength of a synopsis and the opening chapters. A publisher, liking what he saw, would then probably ask to see the whole book before making an offer, although there are occasional high-profile exceptions. However, your completed book could easily be turned down, no matter how keen the publisher was on your initial submission.

Writing an entire book without the security of knowing it will be published is not something that generally happens in non-fiction writing. In fact, a non-fiction book is easier to sell, although you will still need a variation of the synopsis – a book proposal. If you have no track record, a publisher might also like to see a chapter or two to get a feel for your style.

How to Write a Book Proposal

Writing a full book proposal may sound like a chore, but it enables you to see if you genuinely do have the material for a book. It is also much less of a chore than writing an entire book, then hawking it round publishers unsuccessfully and with massive postage costs.

A book proposal will generally consist of:

- A covering (title) page.
- An introduction, outlining the target market for your book.
- A chapter-by-chapter breakdown.
- A survey of competing books.

You will also need a covering letter and an SAE. You may find other advice as to how to lay this out, but this is an approach that has worked for me and for other writers I know. Let's examine each of these elements in turn, but not in the order in which you would present your finished proposal. There is a logic to this, if you will bear with me.

A Survey of Competing Books – Looking at the Market

Once you have the idea for a book, let it marinate for a while whilst you jot down a few notes. It is not a bad idea to set aside a notebook specifically for this job. I normally use a reporter's notebook until I feel that the idea is beginning to take shape and is likely to become a viable project. Then I transfer what I've got into a more substantial A4 notebook, where I can start adding more ideas and details.

When you have got an idea of what your book is about, then it is vital that you check out the market to see what other books exist. If there are too many competing books, then you could well be wasting your time and industrial quantities of stamps.

For instance, I recently had an idea for a book that would look at pseudo-science from a layperson's point of view. I wanted to debunk myths and point out that, in an age when more people believe in ghosts than God, some people were believing anything and buying expensive snake oil to go with it. I thought I was on to a winner, but as soon as I investigated the market, it was obvious that the field was absolutely stuffed full of debunking books. Realizing that the field was too crowded meant dropping the idea straight away, with only a handful of notes and a few hundred words written. Of course, it is disappointing not to get to develop an idea, but by the same token it is better to drop the idea at that stage than to invest days of work into a proposal that stands little hope of seeing the light of day.

It doesn't matter if there is already a small number of books similar to the one you propose. Of course potential publishers are going to want to know about possible competition, but it may not be a problem. It can also help you to see exactly into what niche your book would fit. There may be plenty of books on advanced pole-vaulting, for instance, but nothing for the beginner, so you could slant your idea accordingly.

If you do come across a small number of similar books, include a brief synopsis of each book in this part of your final proposal. Don't criticize the 'opposition' too heavily, but do indicate how your book is different. For example:

Advanced Tiddlywinks by Acton Trussell
This is an excellent book, but it automatically assumes that the tiddlywinks player has a full understanding of the jargon and basic techniques of the game. It also gives strategies that require the kind of skill that can only be built up over years. The book also lacks diagrams. I expect that beginners would buy my book as it would be more accessible. There is a bigger potential market for books for the beginner than for the more advanced player.

This quick critical examination of potential opposition also gives you a chance to restate some of your book's marketing strengths. Doing this in the 'illogical' order will allow you to see if your idea is marketable before you start working on the proposal in depth.

Title

Titles are far more important for books than they are for articles. After all, you hope that bookshops will stock your book. Potential purchasers are going to look at the book cover: the title, picture and blurb should entice them into the first page or two.

If you can come up with a catchy title, then this is great. Some books will sell themselves on their title alone. *How to Build a Better life by Stealing Office Supplies* is a wonderful title – I bought a copy of the book to give to a friend without knowing what was in the book at all. *Getting the Buggers to Behave* was probably bought by every frazzled schoolteacher in the country. Another couple I came across whilst researching this chapter were *Great Lies to Tell Small Kids* and *I'm Too Young to be Seventy – And Other Delusions* (the first is ideal for new parents and plenty of seniors will be unwrapping a copy of the second on their seventieth birthdays). Yes, they're likely to be humorous and perhaps a bit gimmicky, but what great titles.

Alas, it's not often that you will come up with a great title straight away, but if you do, then so much the better. If not, don't panic. In the notebook that you start for this project, keep several pages spare for recording potential titles. Sometimes you can try too hard and end up with something too gimmicky, especially if you're actually selling something straightforward and unfussy. It's easy to forget that simple titles, such as *How To Look After Your Hamster* (it probably exists, although I didn't check), work well. It tells you exactly what the book is about.

If you do want something fancier, it is a good idea to have a title followed by an explanation. *Stand and Deliver: And Other Brilliant Ways to Give Birth* is much catchier than *Alternative Methods of Childbirth*. *Ukulele Breakthrough – Helping Yourself Go from Lonely Strummer to Life-of-the-Party* beats *Playing the Ukulele: Beginner to Intermediate*. Strangely, there is no copyright on titles, although I can't see the point of giving your book the same title as an existing work.

At this stage, the publisher probably only wants an indicative title. Between commissioning and preparing for publication a book with a similar title to the one you proposed might come onto the market anyway. *Catch-22* famously started life as *Catch-18*, but another book (long forgotten) with the number eighteen in the title came out a month or two beforehand, so the title was changed. It's actually a stroke of luck: *Catch-22* is a better title. If in doubt, go for a provisional title that is informative, such as *Oliver Cromwell: A Life*, *Goat-Keeping for Smallholders* or *Cruising the Canals of France*. You and the publisher can bat ideas around at a later stage. Above all, don't get hung up about it. At worst, take your dilemma down to the pub and see if your friends can come up with suggestions bribed only by the vague promise of a free drink.

An Introduction

Once you are beginning to get a feel for the ground your book is going to cover, then it's not a bad idea to try to write the introduction to your book proposal. You will probably want to alter it once you've done a chapter-by-chapter breakdown, but I think the advantage in writing the introduction now is that it helps you to focus your thoughts on the book as a whole. Your introduction needs to answer two main questions:

Who Will Buy this Book? It is tempting to answer 'anyone', especially if you're writing a general book on dieting, cookery or keep-fit. Unfortunately, that's too vague. It is also simply not true. If everyone was likely to buy your book, you would sell around 60 million copies in the UK alone. You won't. Only a handful of books sell more than a million copies.

Say, for instance, you were to write the biography of a well-known footballer. It is unlikely to appeal to anyone not interested in football. It may even only appeal to those people who support the club he plays for. If you're trying to sell the book to a publisher, you need to provide some statistics that show that there is a market. How many people watch live football? How many watch it on the telly? How many hits a week does the club's website get? Is the player an international, in which case supporters of England (or whoever) might be interested in the book. How many people are in the official England (or whoever) supporters' club? Is there a similar book about a similar player? If so, how many copies did that sell?

Why Will They Buy the Book? It is not enough to say that they will buy the book because they're interested in football. Try selling a book on a Manchester United player to a Manchester City fan (unless it's about Dennis Law). There have to be specific reasons why someone should want your book, and these might include:

- There is no other book on the subject.
- Every other book on the subject is at a different level.
- Every other book on the subject is deadly serious.
- Every other book on the subject is entirely academic.
- Your subject is the latest big thing and it will be in a publisher's best interests to get in early.
- There is a great deal of interest in this field.

Chapter-by-Chapter Breakdown

Unless you are extremely logical, deciding on what goes into a book and in what order is extremely difficult. You might be lucky and be able to divide your book into chapters at an early stage in its development and from the chapter headings decide what you will cover at each stage. However, if you're not blessed with that degree of logic (and few of us are) and seem merely to be piling up ideas without any structure, then there are ways round this. One is to use index cards: as ideas occur to you, you can jot them down on separate cards. Don't push the process, just allow it to happen. Spend some time every day, adding ideas to cards. Then when you feel you have enough material to at least make a start on imposing order, try organizing the cards into chapters. You can, of course, use the brainstorming and mind-mapping techniques discussed in Chapter 2.

Whenever I start to organize ideas, two important things happen. One is that I come up with yet more ideas during the process of organization. Then, when I've got something that is beginning to look vaguely like the structure of a book, it becomes clear that there are topics or themes or ideas that I have omitted – often glaringly obvious ones. So I can then start plugging the gaps; once that's done I then start thinking of potential chapter headings.

The underlying principle is that if you are not a natural planner (I'm not), you still have to come up with a means of getting your work into a logical order before you start work on it. Once you have the ideas for each chapter, you can then start writing a brief synopsis of what each chapter will contain. A paragraph or two will be enough. If you're not sure yet how each chapter will be organized then you can always use bullet points.

Your Qualifications for Writing this Book

You also need to convince a publisher that you are qualified to write this book. Most publishers will be looking for subject expertise and some experience of writing for publication, although the expertise is probably more important than the writing. It may be that your usual CV, or a mildly adapted version, is perfectly adequate for this. If you have worked in the field about which you are writing for some time, this might be seen as qualification enough.

In that case, simply include it with your proposal. If your CV doesn't contain enough of the right kind of experience, then you are probably best leaving it aside and including a few paragraphs about yourself in the written proposal. There is no need to go overboard here – you are simply looking to show the publishers that you can write the book you are proposing. To an extent they will be able to see that from the proposal; if you've written it in an inviting and informative way, then your battle is half won.

Make sure that your little biography is relevant. The fact that you sky-dived for charity may be fascinating, it may mark you out as bold (or mad), but it is not relevant to your book on training racing pigeons (unless you train them by taking them with you when you leap from the aeroplane). Boasting that you can write because your friend Ethel likes your Christmas Round Robin isn't going to impress the editorial department. Keep it relevant, sensible and practical.

SENDING OUT YOUR BOOK PROPOSAL

Once you have checked your proposal thoroughly, do the usual trick of putting it away in a drawer for a few weeks, so that you can look at it again with a critical eye. When you have given it a final once-over, it is time to start sending it out. If you have an agent, they will do this for you, but we will assume here that you don't have one.

Whilst your proposal is languishing in a drawer, you can use the time to build up a list of potential targets. There is no point in sending your proposal to a publisher who has something too similar to yours – I have accidentally done that before now, so do as I say and not as I have done. It is just a waste of paper, stamps and effort.

Likewise, if your work is likely to be a short, snappy text-based book, there is no point in sending the idea to a publisher who produces lavish coffee-table books stuffed with glorious pictures. Publishers, like editors, are forever receiving material that is entirely unsuitable. Poetry presses get ideas for workshop manuals and imprints specializing in the history of car marques get *How To Look After Your Fluffy Bunny*. Try to get it as accurate as possible. Nor is there any use in trying the 'I know you normally only publish books on washing-machine maintenance, but I think my book based on my Aunty Mabel's diaries would be just the thing for your publishing company to take off in a new direction' approach.

Use a sensible mixture of library and bookshop browsing to find publishers of titles where you think your book might fit. Also refer to the various writers' handbooks – double-checked against publishers' Internet sites. Eventually you should have a decent list of potential publishers.

Send your proposal to several publishers at a time. Publishers, of course, would like to think that they are the only ones to receive a copy of your proposal. This would be fair enough if publishers responded rapidly, but they can take weeks and often several months to reply (or sometimes fail to reply at all, despite the SAE). As publishers turn you down, just keep working through your list. Keeping accurate records is important.

There is always the possibility that more than one publisher will be interested. This isn't a problem. In fact, it puts you in a strong position as you can then try to negotiate a better deal, or failing that, go with the publisher who you think would do your book the most justice.

The Covering Letter

Your proposal needs a covering letter. You will see that there is some repetition between the covering letter and the proposal; a covering letter is almost a mini-proposal anyway. You are trying to tempt the publisher into eating the whole box of chocolates by giving him or her a couple to sample. Essentially, your letter needs to contain a brief résumé of the following information:

* What the book is about.
* Who the book is for.
* Why you are the right person to write it.
* An idea of how long the book should be.
* If you can, it is also a good idea to show the publisher where it would fit into their catalogue – could it be part of a series, for instance?
* If you can include something in your letter that will grab the editor/publisher's attention (without being too gimmicky) so much the better.
* Don't forget the SAE.

Your beautifully written proposal and snappy covering letter are now winging their way around publishers. Many will say 'no', but you only need one publisher to show faith in you. Whilst you are waiting for the replies to come in, start work on another project – another book proposal, an article, sending off a couple of fillers. Above all, get more ideas out into the marketplace. A lot of publishers are about to turn you down and you need to have a fresh project in mind should this one not bear fruit.

Covering Letter

Dear Mrs Publisher,

Stop the Packaging Nightmare

Sixty thousand people are taken to hospital each year due to injuries received from packaging. *Stop the Packaging Nightmare* is a book designed to help people avoid such accidents.

It is aimed at people in the home or workplace who have to deal with packaging as part of their everyday lives. Professional gift-wrappers, Internet auctioneers, mail order shoppers and supermarket shelf-stackers are just some of the millions of people who have to deal with potentially lethal packaging.

I have worked in packaging accident prevention for several years and have written several articles for *Packaging Safety Monthly*. I am in demand for packaging safety seminars throughout the country.

I see the book as being about 50,000 words, and suggest it would fit into your 'Safety Tips for Home and Work' series.

I enclose a full proposal for *Stop the Packaging Nightmare* and a stamped, addressed envelope for your convenience.

Yours sincerely (or faithfully if you can't get a name),

Penelope Witter

Example: A Book Proposal

This is the proposal for a book I wrote a few years ago that was published by RoutledgeFalmer as Learning to Teach Adults: An Introduction. *It does not include the section on competing books out of deference to my fellow authors and because that is so out of date as to be irrelevant.*

Why We Need this Book

Pundits keep on telling us that the future of education lies in modern technologies. Information Technology is the key to adult learning. Open and distance learning will supplant traditional forms of education and we will all be free to learn at our own pace using the telephone, the Internet and the television.

We have all these things already and, yes, we do use them in the teaching of adults. But when it comes down to it, adults want to come to a class to learn; they don't want to be an anonymous part of a technological process. They want to socialize, interact with like-minded people and know that they can rely on their tutor at any given time. These technologies may supplement classroom-based adult education, but they are never going to replace it.

The key to good learning for adults is a good tutor. Adult classes live and breathe on the efficiency, knowledge, skills and abilities of their tutors, so it is important that people teaching adults know what they are doing. This book is about how to develop those skills.

There are several books available on the subject of teaching adults in further, higher and adult education. So why should we need another?

- Many of the books available on the subject seem to assume that their readers have an academic background.
- Not all teachers of adults have an academic background. Many of them are hobbyists passing on skills gained from practical experience. Workplace trainers are normally selected for experience and knowledge and not necessarily for their academic prowess or paper-based qualifications.
- Many of the available books are simply too dry, so even if the reader has come to the teaching of adults via a traditional educational route, they are uninviting and unappetizing.
- Books that start with a first line like 'The human activity which we call "education" is largely based in our society on the related processes known as "teaching" and "learning"' are hardly designed to grip the reader from the off.
- Most of the books are too long and look like text books. This book aims to be short, snappy and the kind of book that can be picked up and read easily, rather than pored over in a library.

There is no reason why a book should not be readable. After all, teaching adults is an exciting job, so why shouldn't reading about it be exciting too?

Who this Book is For

This book is for the person who is going to be teaching adults for the first time or who has only recently started to do so. It would also be useful to anyone who is already teaching in another sector (schoolteaching, for example, or as a refresher to people who are returning to teaching after a career gap).

It is aimed primarily at the person teaching in a Further Education College or at a local Adult Education Centre. It would also be useful for anyone involved in the teaching or training of adults in any context for the first time. It is not linked to any particular subject, so it can be of use to anyone no matter what subject they teach. Furthermore, it will contain practical examples from a wide range of subjects, thereby including many potential readers.

What this Book Is

- A useful primer and source of ideas for people who are about to start teaching adults.
- A practical handbook of advice, ideas, hints and information for anyone who has recently begun to teach adults.
- A reminder of good practice for those with more experience.
- A short, readable guide for anyone involved in the education of adults.

Chapter 1 – The Adult as a Learner

In this chapter, we examine some of the basic ideas of adult education and training. We shall see how it differs from the teaching of children. This chapter will lay the foundations for the rest of the book and will consist of two short sections.

What is an Adult?
Before we start to look at the mechanics of teaching, it is worth thinking a little about what the word adult means. So, first of all, how do we know when someone is an adult? How do we define what an adult is? Why are adults different to children?

The Adult as a Learner
Most of our experiences of education are as children, receiving an education, rather than either as adults or as teachers. What did we like or dislike as children? How has this affected us as adult learners?

Adults come to classes equipped with experience of education. They also have different levels of life experience, knowledge, commitment, confidence, motivation, social backgrounds, educational achievements, ages and attitudes. How do we cope with all this? What effect does it have on how we deal with adults? This section will take each of these themes in turn and guide the reader through some ideas about what to expect from his or her class.

Chapter 2 – What Is Learning?

This chapter will be divided into four sections. It will contain the most 'academic' material of the book.

Defining Learning
First, we will deal with the difficult subject of defining learning. Once we have looked at various definitions, we will examine what these mean in practice. We will learn about the concepts of psycho-motor, cognitive and affective skills and the various ways in which people learn in each of these domains.

Example: A Book Proposal *continued*

Motivation
It is also important to understand what motivates adult learners and what their needs are as learners. We will look at some of the key ideas in motivation and how they apply to teaching a group of adults.

Learning Styles
Everyone has his or her own preferred style of learning. Some students like a theoretical approach; others prefer a practical, hands-on style of learning. There are also students who represent every shade of grey in-between.

Blocks to Learning
Often adults find it difficult to learn something new. Sometimes what they are learning jars against previous knowledge, or they are anxious. Importantly, we will look at what factors act as blocks to learning, including emotional factors, and what can be done to overcome them.

Chapter 3 – Learning in Groups

We have now seen how individuals learn, but as we are teaching adults in groups, we need to know something of the way they learn in groups. Every group goes through a process in order to establish itself as a group. We examine these stages and processes and what implications they have for the teacher of adults. We will also see how the dynamics of the group can be changed by seating arrangements, and so on. We shall look at how to manage the group as a teacher in order to allow all members of the group to benefit from the course.

Now that we've got some idea of how adults learn, we are ready to start planning our course.

Chapter 4 – Teaching Methods

Many people who are new to teaching adults can only draw on their experience as learners at school and university. This chapter aims to broaden the reader's knowledge of what teaching methods are available. Each teaching technique will be explained and the reader will be helped to evaluate which methods might be appropriate to his or her subject. The methods to be covered would include: assignments, brainstorming, buzz-groups, case studies, debates, demonstrations, discussion, display, explanation, field trips, ice-breakers, interviews, lectures, lecturettes, open and distance learning, panels, problem solving, projects, questioning, role-plays, seminars and snowballing.

How to use questioning is often a problem for new teachers, so we will look at the use of questioning techniques (open and closed questions) and teaching style.

This chapter has been deliberately placed before the chapter on planning as newer tutors tend to focus on the micro-level rather than on programme planning. The positioning of this chapter at this stage would encourage them to experiment and explore new methods and ideas.

Chapter 5 – Planning

This chapter will be divided into two sections – course planning and lesson planning.

Course Planning
Planning a course is one of the hardest parts of a new teacher's job. Even if a syllabus already exists, the teacher of adults has to think of ways in which this can be turned into a proper course. We will examine what certain keys terms, such as aims, objectives and learning outcomes mean and why it is important to use them in planning.

Lesson Planning
Once you have established a general course plan, you need to decide how to break this down into individual lessons. We will look at practical examples of lesson plans.

Chapter 6 – Resources for Teaching and Learning

New technology means that the resources available to both teachers and students are constantly changing. We will look at the range of resources available, how they are used and their suitability for different kinds of teaching and subjects. The resources covered will include cassette tape recorders, the chalkboard/blackboard, computers (including the use of the Internet), flipcharts, games, text books, handouts, radio and television, slides, the overhead projector and video, with practical tips on how and when to use them.

We will also look in detail at how to prepare worksheets and other home-produced teaching material, including audio-visual aids, in order to enable the teacher to enhance the learning experience.

Chapter 7 – Assessment and Evaluation

This chapter will be divided into two sections. Assessment and evaluation are often confused; the two terms will be defined before moving on to the main body of the chapter.

Assessment
The first will deal with how to assess student progress. If a course is vocational, there may well be a formal way of assessing student progress. If it is a leisure class, students still need to know that they are making some kind of progress and this section will discuss possible ideas for doing this. We will also look at the current trend towards the accreditation of courses and to what extent this is or is not a good idea for the newer tutor.

Evaluation
The second section will look at means by which the teacher can assess his or her work in the classroom. It will include ideas for receiving feedback from the group and methods of self-evaluation.

Chapter 8 – Student Participation

Leading on directly from the previous chapter where we have discussed student involvement in the evaluation process will be the idea of involving students in the whole process of the class. We will look at the concept of 'negotiating'; defining what we mean by it, then examining ways in which students can become immersed in the whole process of determining their course content and teaching and learning methods. Some students can present us with greater problems than others. We have all come across

Example: A Book Proposal *continued*

the shrinking violet or the person who wants to dominate the group and we will learn some techniques for dealing with these kinds of people.

A course in which students feel their opinions and ideas are important is a successful class. Learning how to negotiate what students learn and how they learn is an integral part of that process.

Chapter 9 – Domestic Business

In order to run a successful class there are many items of basic good housekeeping that fall on the teacher. This chapter will examine such matters as record-keeping, health and safety, attendance, the preparation of a teaching box, advertising and all the other peripheral aspects of teaching that go into maintaining a successful adult education teaching career.

Attendance
We will suggest ways in which the teacher can maintain good attendance at the class and will identify a range of techniques that are available to him/her to avoid student dropout.

Advertising
The tutor who contributes to the advertising of his or her course often stands a much greater chance of attracting enough students to run the class. This section will examine ways in which an adult tutor can increase the chances of his/her course succeeding.

Chapter 10 – The First Session

The first meeting of any new group is always a nerve-racking occasion for students and teacher alike and so merits a chapter of its own. There are introductions to be made, new ideas to introduce, and the members of the group have to begin to get to know one another. The first session may well be very different from other lessons in the course in practical terms as well as in terms of content, teaching and so forth.

The chapter will also include a checklist of steps that the reader might take before teaching the first session. It has deliberately been made the last full chapter of the book in order to allow the reader to draw on all the other information in the book before planning their first lesson.

Appendices

Appendix A – Recommended Reading and Viewing
In addition to other books on the teaching of adults, I will suggest films and novels that give an insight into the teaching of adults.

Appendix B – Useful Contacts
This will give the names and addresses of organizations that are of use to the adult education teacher.

Appendix C – Glossary
Definitions for terms used throughout the book.

9 WRITING YOUR BOOK

You recognize the envelope; it's one of your SAEs that have been bouncing back with dreadful regularity. Your book has already been turned down by seventeen publishers and here comes rejection number eighteen. With a heavy heart you tear open the flap ... but hang on ... inside is a warm, fluffy letter from a publisher who likes your idea. Of course, they may not like your idea exactly as you have suggested it, and would like to see changes, or they may like your idea, but need to talk to some other people before making a decision. It's a reason to be cheerful: someone at least thinks you've got a marketable book.

Whatever changes a publisher suggests to you, be prepared to adapt. If they want you to drop the chapter on bee-keeping, then drop it. If they like the idea of 50,000 words rather than the 60,000 you suggested, be prepared to trim. If you are lucky, these preliminary 'yes, but ...' messages will be followed up with the official invitation to have your book published – a contract.

If you don't have an agent, then it is well worth joining the Society of Authors as soon as you have an offer to publish. I have heard of new authors who have turned to the family solicitor for advice on a publishing contract. Publishing contracts are not their normal domain; you need an expert eye, which is where the Society of Authors comes in. They can't be praised highly enough. They will read your contract and if there is anything untoward in it, point it out to you. They will also suggest changes. You can use their advice to try to negotiate a better deal with your publisher. They will certainly agree to anything that is in your mutual interest and some publishers will shift on certain other matters.

At the point of offering a contract publishers will often want to discuss with you when you can get the finished manuscript to them; it is rare that they actually impose a deadline for the simple reason that they want to know that you can make the agreed deadline. If you're not sure how long you need – it is difficult to guess if you have never written a book before and books come in all sorts of lengths anyway – ask what they normally suggest. The date will then be written into the contract.

A Little Caveat

Occasionally when you send out a book proposal you will receive an offer from a publisher suggesting that they will publish your book if you are prepared to contribute to the costs. These publishers often make the most extravagant claims for your work and tend to distort how well your book is likely to do in the market. They can play nasty tricks, such as persuading you that hardback is a better proposition than paperback (it's more expensive) or offering to print 2,000 copies, but failing to state that they're not going to bind those 2,000 copies. Instead of the required number of books, you could find that you have 400,000 sheets of loose paper.

Of course, they don't call themselves 'Vanity Publishers', they use euphemisms such as 'subsidy publishers', 'joint publishing venture' or 'co-contributing publishing partner'. Many are preying on the vulnerable, the gullible and the desperate. Hard though it is, you must try not to fall into any of those categories. If you are that desperate to see your work in print, it is probably a sight cheaper to opt for the self-publishing route, which I discuss briefly in Chapter 10. Bookshops know who the vanity publishers are and don't stock their books.

Writing the Book – Target Setting

So, you've sold your book, ironed out the contract and are ready for the enormous task of writing it. Before you start, pour yourself a drink. You deserve one; you've just sold a book. Be pleased with yourself. You are now about to embark on a long ride of exhilaration and frustration.

Every time you start a book there are two conflicting emotions. One is the excitement of being involved in a big project, a new venture, the buzz of creating something from nothing. The other is that a book is a mountain that needs climbing and, right at the start, the peak of that mountain is shrouded in cloud.

This is why some kind of schedule is important. Don't flagellate yourself if it is proving impossible to stick to what you anticipated, and if you foresee genuine problems in delivering the manuscript on time, contact the publisher at once. They are normally understanding and tend not to be too worried if you are only going to be a week or two behind the agreed date, but they would far rather know where they stand, rather than be sitting there waiting for your manuscript to hit their desks, wondering why they haven't heard from you.

Dividing your work up into manageable chunks is vital. A book, even a comparatively short one, is a lot of work. When a publisher gives you a dead-line, it often seems an age away when you first get it. However, the law of 'famine or feast' always means that having had nobody interested in your work, suddenly you're in high demand. Work has to be prioritised. What looked like nine months in which to write the book becomes six, then five, then four. Suddenly, like Christmas, the deadline is upon you. It's even harder if you are holding down another job at the same time.

Writing a book is like eating sickly chocolate – it is best to try to nibble away at a small amount each day. As soon as you get your deadline, divide the time that you have into three chunks: one for note-taking and research; one for writing; then an interval of a few weeks before the final segment, which is looking at the book from a detached viewpoint and bringing it up to a publishable standard. Also allow for slippage time. Even as I am typing these words, I am aware that I am about three weeks behind my own personal schedule. Hopefully, the bit of 'cushion-time' in my timetable will stop me panicking too much.

Of course, this division of time is not set in stone. For instance, you might like to research the material for one chapter, then write that chapter before moving onto the next and so on. My point is that you have to allow time for each step in the process of writing a book.

It is also impossible to say how much you need to devote to each part of this process – that depends entirely on you and the kind of book you are writing. If you already have notebooks full of research material, then you may not have to do much preparation before you start writing. If you write quickly, then you may not need as much time for this as a more methodical and painstaking writer, who might in turn find that he or she has to spend less time at the checking stage than the bull-in-a-china-shop writer who hacks thing out quickly, then has to do a lot of rewriting.

During the actual writing process, set yourself a daily word target. Again, this is highly personal and will also depend on your deadline. Anything from 500 to 2,000 words is a reasonable daily target, especially as there are going to be days when you just can't work on your book. By that, I don't mean that you will have writers' block, but there will be holidays and days that you have to spend doing other things. Set your daily word target slightly higher than needed if you think you are going to lose whole days in this way. I use the word count facility on my computer to make sure I have met my daily targets – usually around 1,000 words given other commitments. On days that I devote entirely to the writing of a non-fiction book and nothing else, I would expect to write 2,000 to 2,500 rough, unpolished words.

BRINGING ORDER TO YOUR WORK

If you are highly methodical, you might be able to start on page 1 of your book and continue until you get to the end. If so, you need no help in being organized and the rest of us are enormously jealous. There are several reasons why writing from A–Z doesn't work for everyone. Most of us are not that organized, for a start. Many writers like to get plenty of words down on the page or screen and then play around with them (the method I use). This means that they rattle away at the keyboard, producing thousands of words, whilst Mr Methodical is still on page 2. They then spend ages cutting and pasting their work, trying to remove any duplication and polishing their sentences.

Meanwhile, Mr Methodical (still plodding) finishes and has only two mistakes to put right. Hey-ho.

It may be instructive for me to explain how I actually wrote this book. I do not do this to flaunt what I've done, but to help anyone who feels disorganized and floundering, and to let them know that there are ways of doing it. As soon as I had a contract I started a large A4 notebook that would be dedicated to this project. Using the book I jotted notes and ideas and even wrote a few paragraphs at random. Just about everywhere I went the book went with me, so that at odd moments on trains or in cafés, I could add something.

I made no effort to bring any order to my notes – I had a framework in the shape of my book proposal anyway, even though I have subsequently subdivided some of the proposed chapters that I felt were too unwieldy. Instead of typing up my work chapter by chapter, I made smaller separate computer files that dealt with individual topics – little sections, if you like. Then, whenever I came across another note that related to that topic, I could add it into the relevant file on the computer. When I had most of the relevant elements for each chapter, I then pasted them up into a chapter. If the chapter then proved unwieldy compared to my original proposal, I subdivided it.

The cut and paste facility that comes with word processing software means that it is easy to bring order to chaos; a few linking sentences to make sections flow into one another and you have a complete first full draft. Of course, it is perhaps easier with a book like this, consisting of a series of small topics, to adopt this approach. If you require narrative flow, it is harder. The biography of a famous actor, for instance, might not lend itself to this treatment. However, if you embrace the general philosophy, then you soon realize that you don't always have to write Chapter 2 before you write Chapter 3, which is wonderfully liberating for the disorganized amongst us.

Tone and Content

To get the tone of your book right, it's not a bad idea to try to conjure up a picture of who your reader might be. Is this a book for beginners? How much would a reader have to know about the subject before coming to your book? Best of all is to identify a particular individual you know and write with him or her in mind.

I always try to find an intelligent layperson to read my books when they're finished to see if they are happy with what I've written. They don't have to agree with it; I just want them to flag up any parts that were confusing or vague or contradictory or nonsensical. I'm not asking them to pick up spelling mistakes (although they often do), but to give me an appraisal of the book in terms of its readability.

It is unlikely that the book you have written will match up 100 per cent with the proposal you sent out. Publishers will not normally mind this, provided you have not deviated too far from the original agreed proposal. They accept the fact that, whilst you are writing a book, information changes and new facts come to light. They also realize that sometimes what seemed like the most logical order for a book at proposal stage does not seem logical when it comes to writing. Some parts of the book that looked as though they were worth an entire chapter might not pan out that way; similarly, some chapters might need subdividing. Don't worry too much about this – if in doubt, talk to the publisher.

The last thing I do is read it through myself. I do this twice, trying to leave a gap of several weeks between each stage. The first is a quick read, where I try to identify any obvious duplications or omissions. I then rectify these and put the manuscript to one side. Then, just before I send it out, I give the manuscript a final check and try to spot as many mistakes as I humanly can, but inevitably some will slip through the net. I try not to start changing anything else too much, unless there is something that leaps off the page at me as being awful. You can fiddle with a manuscript forever, but at some point you have to let go.

WHEN THE BOOK IS FINISHED

Eventually, when you have your finished manuscript and have checked it as thoroughly as you can, send it off with a certificate of postage. Most publishers want a hard (paper) copy of your book as well as a copy on disk, although you might just be asked to send it as an email attachment. Just stick with what they ask. Receipt of your finished manuscript should, if your contract stipulates, trigger the next payment.

My friend Peter van der Linden calls this the stage when the publisher takes out all of your mistakes and puts in some of their own. You can't pick up all your mistakes and now somebody at the publishers should begin work on editing your book. They are looking to make your book as good as it possibly can be. Sometimes you may be asked to rewrite some sections; more usually, an editor is giving the manuscript some tweaks. At this stage, you might decide to reorder some chapters, but it's unlikely that you have got huge amounts of work left to do. If your book is running a little too long, it might need some additional trimming (always easier than padding) and you might be short of a diagram or two (where appropriate). However, often the book now disappears into a black hole and you are simply waiting around wondering what is happening.

If you are providing an index to the book, this is often the point at which it is done. Normally, you will create the index yourself, as the cost of indexing is generally charged to the author and subtracted from the advance payment. You can use the computer to index, but it's a process fraught with difficulty and you are better off preparing the subjects for your index manually. Unless your book is highly academic, it is simpler to stick to main subjects and people for the index. I usually take a highlighter pen to my spare copy of the submitted manuscript and mark up topics that I think are relevant. Once I've done this, I then type up the list and simply put it into alphabetical order using the facility on the computer; I add page numbers at proof stage.

If you don't hear anything from the publishers, don't worry and don't hassle them. After all, they probably didn't hassle you when you were doing the writing. Eventually they will send back to you the proofs for correcting. If you were to compare the proofs to the manuscript you submitted, there will almost certainly be minor changes. The editor will have de-mangled a sentence or made a cut or an alteration. It is unlikely that these changes will be particularly substantial, or you would have been consulted.

Your job now is not to quibble about minor alterations, but to read over the proofs to look for any mistakes. You will be given a deadline for this and you must meet it. You have now had a period away from the work and should come to the task with fresh eyes. Again, don't try to alter the text too much – in fact, if you alter it too much you may incur typesetting charges.

You will normally be expected to mark up the text using the British Standards Institution proof-marking system. The *Writers' and Artists' Yearbook* normally contains a copy of these proof marks. If not, ask your publisher if they have a copy – they may even send you one automatically. You may find it easier to do your own version of the proofing in light pencil and then add the official proof marks when you've finished checking. Try not to check too much at a sitting – you will only miss obvious errors. This is also the point at which you should complete your index – you can generally now insert the page numbers against the headings you made whilst the book was being edited.

There are other things that you will be asked for around this time to complete the publishing process.

BLURB

This is the short write-up of the book that usually goes on the back cover and is often included by publishers in their press releases. I am never sure whether it is better for you to write this yourself or to have someone else write it and then tinker with their version. If you establish a good relationship with whoever is doing your publicity or editing, then you can probably work something out between you.

Condensing the whole of a book into a hundred words or so is quite a skill. Often it is worth returning to your book proposal to see if you can use parts of it as a basis. If the blurb is written for you (the case with larger publishers), make sure that you can have some sort of approval over it. Again, as most publishers are looking to maximize sales, they are more than likely to encourage cooperation between their publicity department and you. It serves neither party if you fall out.

BIOGRAPHICAL DETAILS

This is the horrible part. You need to condense who you are into a couple of sentences that must promote your book and, at the same time, not sound like vainglorious boasting. Either you'll be struggling for words or stumped as to what to leave out.

It looks like the easiest job in the world. However, you are unlikely to get the luxury of a well-known novelist's résumé. Exclude mention of your domestic affairs – we probably don't want to know that you keep seven hedgehogs as household pets, unless, of course, your book is about hedgehogs. If you have a CV, print off a copy and take a highlighter pen to any bits you think are relevant, then condense that information as far as you can without turning it into a telegram. There is nothing wrong with something as brief as:

Penelope Witter is a safety expert who understands the dangers of packaging. She is making it her mission to make packaging safer for everyone.

Essentially, you want readers to know that you have the credentials to write this book and thus give them the confidence to buy it.

COVER

You may also be sent a copy of the proposed cover. If you're lucky, you might have some say in the cover design, but this is unlikely if you are an unknown author. It is in the publisher's interest to have as attractive a cover as possible. Publishers want to sell your book just as much as you do. You may have invested a great deal of time in your work; so have they. You have both spent money on the enterprise. They also have expertise – after all, they are probably well-versed in the publishing game; you're the newcomer.

You can occasionally get a little bit of leeway on the cover. On the other hand, many non-fiction books are part of a series, so the cover will have to have the look and feel of a book in that series. This may be no bad thing for your book sales. People like to buy what is familiar and if the publishers have branded a series of books so as to make them readily identifiable to potential purchasers, then this is likely to act in your favour.

DEDICATIONS, THANKS AND OTHER AUTHORIAL SPOUTING

Almost no book is written without input from someone other than the author. Very often, it is the spouse/partner/significant other who does a huge amount of unseen work. Without them your book wouldn't see the light of day. Some books are therefore cluttered with all sorts of twee little endearments such as 'for Choochy-Face, who was there during the deepest moments of my despair to catch my dreams and set them back on course'. Most people reading twaddle like this will probably want to take out a death warrant on Choochy-Face and are probably going to be put off reading your book.

Give genuine thanks to those people who deserve it. If you can add in a touch of humour, fine – it's an indication that your book will not be stodgy. Dedicate your book to someone you love, or failing that a tobacco, alcohol or drugs manufacturer whose products have helped you stay at your desk.

FREE COPIES

Would you believe that the number of free copies given to an author by the publisher can be as low as just six? That would give you one copy to use 'in rough' as it were, one to put away in the loft in brown paper for posterity and four to give away to family and friends. Often, friends will be surprised that you are unable to give away more copies. Simply explain to them the state of affairs and you may find them buying your book. Good for you; that's another sale.

On the other hand, there are those people who genuinely helped in the writing of a book. They should get a free copy. Often, a publisher will provide a couple of extra copies to give to people who have given their time to a project. Most publishers won't balk at a few copies and will often send them directly to the person concerned, but if you start trying to get handfuls of books for free, they are not going to play your game.

THE LAUNCH PARTY AND OTHER PUBLICITY

You are unlikely to get a launch party unless you organize one yourself. All those scenes of London literati getting stuck into canapés and champagne are more the stuff of film than they are of reality.

If your book is of local interest, it may be worth organizing an event at a nearby hotel or bookshop – especially if the bookshop is one of the dwindling band of genuine independents. Don't overdo it; a minor buffet, some wine and soft drink will be enough. Make sure that you invite the local press; you need as much publicity as you can get. If you are lucky, your publisher might chip in to help with the costs, but don't hold your breath. The publisher's publicity department is probably far more concerned with trying to get your book reviewed in the right places.

Publishers' publicity departments will often send authors a questionnaire to help them with the marketing of the book. A typical questionnaire will ask if you have any press or relevant professional contacts, if you know of specialist publications at which the book could be targeted and any local connections you have. Don't just rush at it. Leave it to one side and jot down notes against each heading. Then, when you have thought of all the possible avenues that the publisher could use to push your book, return the completed form. This is important. The publicity department's job is to sell your wares, but if you leave the entire process up to them, there is no way in which your book will sell well. Publishers like authors who help to sell their books.

Often, at this stage, you may realize that there are potential spin-off articles from your book – if your book isn't an amalgamation of your articles anyway. I once got a commission by phone on the basis of a book I had written and was essentially asked to amalgamate the first two chapters into a shorter piece, so I had my young editor, who was doing the publicity, to thank for a handsome cheque. If you do have opportunities for spin-off articles, make sure that at the end of your article you write something like 'Penelope Witter is a packaging safety specialist, whose latest book *Stop the Packaging Nightmare* is published by Safety Books'.

The publicity for a book can be fun. Count yourself lucky if you are interviewed on local radio or by your local newspaper. Occasionally, you might even get on national radio or TV, but normally only if you have got something a little out of the ordinary. On the few occasions that I have been asked, I've regarded such things as a bit of fun whilst promoting my book. It also gets you out of the house, gives you potential material for your articles and you occasionally meet well-known people you would not normally come into contact with. As for how many books it sells I have no idea, but at least you can then say your book has been featured on radio and TV.

10 OTHER WAYS TO MAKE MONEY

Few writers live solely on their income from writing. It is often a good idea to have more than one string to your bow; flexibility is important. We have already seen that being able to turn your hand to several different types of writing is useful. It is also a good idea to develop a range of complementary skills that can enhance both your reputation and your income.

TEACHING

Teaching writing is often used by writers as a way to generate additional income. Assuming that anyone reading this book is looking to develop a career in writing, rather than in teaching, I will limit myself in these few pages to the part-time opportunities that exist for writers.

If you already have teaching experience, especially if you are a qualified teacher, then teaching writing is a logical adjunct to writing. If you are not a trained teacher, then there are still opportunities for you, but you need to be aware that teaching looks easier than it is. Your lessons need to be well-planned and structured. You will find that you need to spend a great deal of time building up a bank of useful materials.

If you are writing more or less full-time, it is often surprising how little contact you have with the outside world. Teaching can be an excellent way of meeting people and helping to take care of the social aspects of work that are often missing from a writer's life.

Adult and Further Education

Over the years colleges and education authorities have provided a broad mix of classes in subjects ranging from modern languages to yoga, computing to Chinese brush painting. More recently, creative writing classes have become a regular feature of community education brochures. Adult and community learning is a great area in which to find work. You don't necessarily have to have a teaching qualification, although increasingly it is expected, so there may be opportunities for you to gain a part-time qualification in further education teaching, which is useful in its own right. Students tend to be well-motivated and keen.

If you are looking for work in this sector, check out your local adult education brochures and find out if any similar courses exist. Don't worry too much if they do – personnel come and go and organizers always need a bank of part-time tutors even if they can't use you immediately. Equally, if there is a gap in the market a well-written approach might pay dividends.

Write to the person responsible either for your geographic area or for your subject. As well as including a CV, it is also worth attaching a series of ideas for courses. Each idea should consist of a title and then a paragraph or two describing the content of the course – almost like the blurb for a book. The best time to approach centre managers and programme leaders is around March or April; they will just be starting to think about their autumn programmes. A professional package is manna to most adult education organizers. They are often keen for something new to include in their programme. For example:

Writing Articles for Magazines

Writing articles for magazines is a great way of breaking into print and can be personally and financially rewarding. This course is a practical introduction, full of help and advice and with plenty of opportunities for you to try out your own ideas. We will look at where and how to find ideas, how to write them up and where to sell your work.

Writing a Non-Fiction Book

Although many people would love to write a novel, you stand a much greater chance of being published with a non-fiction book. This course will take you through all the stages – from idea to outline, from approaching a publisher with a fully fledged proposal to sitting down and writing. There will be plenty of hand-outs, exercises and information plus a few anecdotes from my own experience.

One area of adult education that is always popular is residential education. As well as colleges funded by local authorities, there are private institutions that provide an atmosphere of calm away from the hurly-burly of modern life. For a practising writer, they offer the possibility to run short, intensive courses on specialist subjects.

If you are happy tutoring would-be writers by distance learning then there are also colleges who operate correspondence or Internet-based courses. These courses often work on the principle that the student sends the tutor a piece of work or posts the work on a secure website for comment. Whilst the flexibility of being able to read and comment on work at a time to suit you is definitely

---

Exercise:

You would like to teach a course entitled 'Making Money from Non-Fiction Writing'. Write a brief course description consisting of a paragraph or two.

appealing, as you can fit your tutoring round other work, it does have its drawbacks. Your comments in print can look cold and harsh when they're not meant to be, you don't have the same relationship with your students as you can in a class as there tends to be little or no face-to-face interaction. Also, distance learning tutors are often poorly paid.

Higher Education

Some universities have Departments of Continuing Education. They offer courses to the general public and are often looking for highly specific courses. Again, funding for the future is not as healthy as it might be and some universities are closing their Continuing Education Departments in order to concentrate on other areas that are better funded by the government and the fee-paying student.

There is, though, a growing number of undergraduate courses that include writing. If you become reasonably proficient as a writer, then it may be possible to find a limited amount of part-time work as a lecturer in writing. Many universities, especially the newer ones, like to employ practising writers as they bring with them practical skills that they can pass on to students.

Going Alone

There is no reason why you couldn't set up and run your own independent courses. If your house is large enough and you have the correct insurance, you could hold them there, although you would be well-advised to find some kind of neutral venue, such as a village or neighbourhood hall. These rarely come cheap; and facilities at hotels and conference centres are even costlier.

You need to think in terms of basic refreshments and possibly even food. With current hygiene regulations, this can be trickier than it looks; to satisfy all the various statutory demands, you might be better off using a small outside catering firm. You also need to decide on a price, which you need to do whilst bearing in mind what is being charged for similar courses in your neighbourhood.

Pricing is always a tricky issue. People who will willingly part with £60 for a hairdo, may begrudge shelling out £30 for the dentist to save a tooth. If you underprice, people can undervalue what you are doing. If you over-price, you may not attract enough people, especially if your venue isn't particularly smart.

Theoretically, with a few strategic adverts and some well-written press releases, you can wait for people to sign up. Unlike teaching in your local Adult Education Centre, all profits are yours. If you attract twelve people, each paying £25 and your costs are £75, then you're earning much more than you would teaching at the local college. It all sounds so easy, you wonder why more writers aren't doing it. The reason is simple – if you only garner six people, you're not going to make a decent profit.

Frankly, unless you are exceptionally entrepreneurial, it is probably not the best way to drum up teaching work. You have to do a huge amount of work and often the response is much poorer than you would have hoped. One of the hardest parts is simply making people aware of your course. Even the smallest Adult Education Centre sends leaflets to doctors' waiting rooms, libraries, local supermarkets and directly to past students. You simply can't cover that kind of ground. Also, each September, adult education regulars are often on the look-out for the next batch of courses in a familiar brochure.

By all means try, but be realistic about your chances of success. If you have got lots of relevant books to try to sell to your students, and can also make a profit on them, then you might think that the economics are more in your favour.

Teaching Isn't Always a Bed of Roses

Be aware that as national pay scales that used to determine tutors' hourly rates have disappeared, or at least been undermined, huge discrepancies in hourly rates of pay have arisen. Many educational providers are simply getting away with paying as little as they possibly can. Even if you are reasonably well paid, the rate for the job is usually based on contact time with the students and teaching is more than just the time spent in front of the class. Those two hours on a Tuesday evening may pay well on an hourly basis, but by the time you have taken into account petrol, preparation time, occasional staff meetings, bits of administration and reading students' work, you might think that you could have spent the time more wisely sending out a few pitches to magazines.

There are certain other pitfalls to consider with teaching. Sometimes, you can find that your own creativity is being sucked away into the teaching rather than your writing. You also need to be able to deal with people from all walks of life, some of whom may demand a great deal of your time and personal resources. On the other hand, these factors should be weighed up against the bonus of having a form of steady income when you're working freelance.

WRITER-IN-RESIDENCE SCHEMES

Not a million miles away from teaching writing are writer-in-residence schemes. These enable a writer to work with a group of people in a given setting to help them produce their own writing. Often, teaching groups is one of the duties involved. Other typical components of a writer-in-residence's brief might be to produce a booklet or magazine or website of writing. You might also be expected to give readings of your own work.

In the main, writer-in-residence schemes are the province of imaginative writers, rather than non-fiction writers. Poets are often popular, perhaps because it is easier for participants to produce a poem (not necessarily a good one) in a short space of time, whereas writing a short story or an article simply takes longer. There is the occasional exception though, and if you are one of that group of writers capable of turning a hand to most forms of writing then you could stand a chance.

TALKS

If you are happy standing up in front of strangers, then it might be worth considering giving talks. It is also a good alternative to teaching adults as it is more flexible than having to devote a set time each week. There are many local groups who often struggle to find new speakers. A covering letter together with the suggested titles and a short description for a handful of titles can bring results. Don't expect to be mown down in the stampede to be booked as a speaker however – these things take time. Often speakers' lists are put together as long as eighteen months in advance. However, once you get onto speakers' circuits, then it is a useful adjunct. You will find that memberships of groups overlap and once you've done a talk to one group, someone will pass the word to another group and so on.

When you give a talk, make the talks centre round subjects that you deal with in your writing if at all possible. If you have a supply of your books (relevant or not) make sure you take them along as well, as this is a golden opportunity to sell a few.

One of the secrets of a good talk is to involve your audience in some way. Even if you are giving an old-fashioned lecture-style talk, you can throw out questions to the audience as you go along so as to break up your spiel. If you can come up with other, more inventive ways of gaining audience participation, even better.

SELF-PUBLISHING

Self-publishing has a long and distinguished history. Such writers as Virginia Woolf, Beatrix Potter, Rudyard Kipling and Horace Walpole all used self-publishing at some point. However, just because some great names grace the pantheon of the self-published, it doesn't mean to say that self-published works will automatically sell well.

Publishing books is an expensive business, although it is less pricey than it once was. There are countless stories of people who follow this route and are left with a garage full of unsaleable books. Of course, when you have tried every publisher you can find and they're still not interested in what you have to offer, you may be tempted. Self-publishing means that you not only write the book, edit it, check it, proofread it and pay someone to print it, but you are then responsible for selling and marketing it. You are now the publisher of your own book, together with all the administration and organization that this requires.

If you do self-publish, it is probably best to work on the principle that you might lose every penny you spend on the project. True, you might also make a good deal more money than if your book were published the traditional way as you should also be making the publisher's profits as well. But don't be seduced into thinking that it is an easy way to make money. Books are notoriously difficult to shift. If you don't believe me, just take a look in your local cheap bookshop, where they often sell off what are known as 'remaindered' titles – essentially publishers' leftovers. Whilst there will be many books by authors you have never heard of, there will be a fair few by names that often grace the best-seller lists. If it is that hard to push books by well-known authors, imagine how hard it is for you to sell your own book.

In the main, there are only two types of book that stand a chance of making money as a self-published venture. These are specialist books and local history. Specialist books can often leapfrog the bookshops system and be sold directly to the people who might most be interested. If you have written a specialist book on your hobby, then you know which magazines might be likely to carry a feature on the book or where to advertise. Similarly, a local history book is unlikely to sell a great deal outside the area it covers, so it is not too difficult to market it to bookshops, gift shops, local societies and so on within the area it covers – often around where the author lives.

The whole process of self-publishing is a complicated one and requires a book of its own to explain the process. Essentially, you now have a dozen roles to play, as well as that of author. Some jobs, such as cover design, page layout, editing, proofreading and, of course, printing can be farmed out to specialists. Your local printer is unlikely to be able to do the job as well as a specialist book printer and will almost certainly be more expensive. You need several estimates and you also need to know how to ask for those estimates as printers have a jargon all their own.

I once heard a fascinating talk on self-publishing. I pass on the wisest words. Printers will normally provide economies of scale – the figures that follow are pure invention, but you should follow the logic. If it costs £2,000 to print 1,000 books, it may cost only £2,500 to print 2,000 as their printing equipment is all set up and it is simply a question of keeping the presses rolling a tad longer. This brings the unit cost down from £2.00 per book to £1.25. By the time you order 10,000 books, the figure might have dropped to fifty pence.

This looks exceedingly tempting. However, you need to ask yourself how many copies you are realistically going to sell. Ten thousand books at fifty pence each will have cost you £5,000. This means that if you only sell 1,000 books, each one you sold will have cost £5.00 to produce in real terms. You would have been far better off accepting the higher unit cost in the first place and opting for the print run of 1,000, which would have set you back £2.00 per book and cost £2,000 overall.

It is obvious that you need to cost out the process rigorously. You could be kissing goodbye to a lot of hard-earned money. Most bookshops will want a hefty discount and some will only buy books on a national basis, leaving local bookshop managers little discretion. If you are planning to sell your book via shops, you will need to obtain an ISBN (International Standard Book Number) and you will also need a barcode. These add to your costs.

However, if you can market your book directly to the buying public – for instance when giving talks to groups on the subject of your book or via a specialist website – then you can keep the entire profit element from each book for yourself. It is not a bad idea to use a name different than your own for your publishing venture. Some buyers still balk slightly at the idea of self-published books, and it puts a small distance between you and your work.

Provided you go into the process with your eyes rather than your wallet wide open, self-publishing could provide you with a useful adjunct to your income. It is an area of publishing that is likely to grow as publishers increasingly buy books that have widespread commercial appeal at the expense of books that sell to smaller markets. Who knows, you could soon find yourself with a little publishing house, producing niche publications to a specialist market.

Of course, you don't have to package what you write as a book in the traditional sense. If you have information that could be sold on a computer disk or as a downloadable e-book, then there are no printing costs involved to speak of. Similarly, you might find that a 32-page pamphlet on a specialist subject, published in A5 format will do the job admirably, can be printed in short runs by your local printer and sells for five times the cost of production.

Self-publishing is often confused with vanity publishing. They are distinct and you have already been warned of the barracudas that infest these waters. As a rule of thumb avoid the vanity press and only self-publish if you are certain you've got a sure-fire success – it is most likely to be local history or some specialist subject, and almost certainly your initial print run will likely be in the region of 500–1,000 copies.

PUBLIC LENDING RIGHT

When you have had a book published, then you are automatically eligible to register for Public Lending Right. PLR distributes money to authors based on the number of times their books are borrowed from libraries. Each withdrawal earns the author a few pence. PLR does not work by monitoring every library in the country, but a sample is used from which to create a fuller picture. You have to earn at least £5.00 from PLR in any one year before they will pay you and there is a maximum payment that currently stands at £6,000. (However, if you get the maximum payment, you're probably doing so well that it'll just feel like a bit of beer money.)

As soon as a book is published and has an ISBN, you can register it for PLR. Don't wait for your publisher to do so on your behalf, that's not their job. You can't expect to earn a fortune from PLR; just consider it a little bit of unexpected income. All freelance writing is about putting different layers of income into your pocket and you'll soon be grateful that all these small amounts from other sources begin to add up (*see* Appendix).

AUTHORS' LICENSING AND COLLECTING SOCIETY

The Authors' Licensing and Collecting Society (ALCS) performs a similar function to PLR, but this income is based on fees from photocopying licensing schemes, German PLR and the re-transmission of TV and radio programmes on cable networks. Whilst the second and third income strand may be irrelevant to you, you may well be eligible for a slice of the photocopying scheme.

It is not to be ignored. Many writers are surprised at the often handsome sums they receive each year from the ALCS. Provided you have published a handful of articles or a book in any given year, it is worth joining the scheme; it is inexpensive to do so and if you are a member of the Society of Authors, membership of ALCS is automatically included. Don't forget that the cost of membership of the ALCS is tax-deductible.

WRITING COMPETITIONS

Poets and short story writers have plenty of competitions open to them. Article or essay-writing competitions are not particularly common, so you need to keep your eyes and ears open. Often, such competitions as do appear are promoted by magazines or the national press.

Winning competitions involves having a slice of luck, as well as skill. Often, the weight of numbers is on your side. Short story writers have few outlets for their talents other than competitions; organize a short story comp and you will be inundated with entries. Non-fiction competitions are often a less-crowded field, so statistically you have a better chance of winning. You can improve your chances by making sure that you follow some simple guidelines, some of these refer to the competition rules and some are tips worth putting into practice:

* Stick to the rules. I once judged a writing competition and around 20 per cent of the entries went unread simply because the entrants had not followed the simple rules that we had laid down.
* If the competition calls for pieces of 800–1,000 words, you stand no chance if you submit something that is patently far too short or far too long. Judges can tell in an instant if a piece of work is obviously of the wrong length. Some competition organizers may even count the words of each entry to ensure that they fall within the guidelines precisely, so it is not even worth going a single word over or under the count.
* Stick to the topic. If the competition asks for a piece of factual reportage on living rough on the streets of Britain, they do not want an opinion piece from you. They want to know what it's like to sleep rough.
* If you need to send in an entry coupon or form cut from a magazine, then send your piece with that form. This might be so that the magazine can sell extra copies to all those people entering a competition. If the judges don't accept photocopies of the form, don't send them; buy an additional copy of the magazine if you must. If there is an entry fee, then you have to pay it. If entries are to be emailed, then you must email them; if they are to be sent by post, send by post.

- Think laterally. If the competition title is something like 'The Twentieth Century' and you are allowed only 2,000 words, it is just too big a topic to be covered fully in the space allowed. In reality, you need seven volumes and a deadline a decade ahead. How could you encapsulate the twentieth century in a short piece? You live in a Victorian house: how about using the inhabitants of the house as indicative of the changes that took place last century?
- It is also probably best to avoid opinion pieces unless the competition calls for them. Judges get tired of the same old arguments being trotted out time after time. These pieces are usually from people who have garnered all their ideas from a tabloid newspaper, are written to sub-GCSE standard, and don't contain one whiff of a new or perceptive idea.
- You are trying to stand out from the crowd, so avoid anything that you have seen covered extensively in the press. Also steer clear of events that are time-bound. There's the old cliché that today's news is tomorrow's fish-and-chip wrapper. And, although editors often like you to hang an article on an anniversary, it is too obvious for a competition piece.
- If the advice for writing articles for magazines is that you need to write 'the same, but different', for competitions, place the emphasis on the word 'different'. You need to stand out from the pack, the last thing you want to be is 'samey'.

Eventually, if you build up a reputation as a writer, you might start being invited to judge competitions. It is not the most lucrative work in the world and you will get to read an awful lot of junk, but it will also help you to sit on the other side of the fence. It is almost like being an editor for a short space of time, without any of the hassles of having to organize print runs, choose pictures and deal with staff. You get to see what doesn't work in an article and learn to avoid it. You also get to see what does work and we can always learn from good examples.

CRITIQUING SERVICE

If you read writers' magazines, you will often see critiquing services advertising in their pages. These outfits, varying from charlatans to the highly professional, offer to read your work and suggest ways of improving it. There is no reason why, once you are reasonably well established, you shouldn't offer the same service. There is no need to advertise your services, you will find that people beat a path to your door. Nearly all of them will want free advice. To begin with, this is flattering. You are a writer and people want to know your opinion. After a while it actually becomes annoying.

People who would never dare ask a doctor to examine them at a dinner party or a plumber to repair their ball-cock for free automatically assume that they can pump you for advice, with no thought that you are giving out professional information that has a financial value. On one occasion, I was phoned out of the blue by someone who, after he had flattered me that I was just the chap he was looking for, asked if he could drop round within the next half-hour with his manuscript to discuss it over a cup of coffee. It was handy as he had to go past my door anyway. I asked him how long his manuscript was and when he told me, I quoted him a fee of several hundred pounds to look at it. On the other end of the telephone was a silence, then:

'You want me to pay?'
'You'd pay a lawyer or an accountant or a plumber.'
'But this is different!'
'How?'
'Well, if that's the way you feel about it ...'

Happily, I never got the manuscript to read. However, it did make me realize that every time I'm asked for advice, I could make money. Now if anyone is looking for advice, instead of feeling put out I tell them my rates, which are based on hourly pay rates for teaching in adult education. If truth be told, I haven't made a great deal this way, but I have picked up the occasional cheque and have certainly nipped a few pointless conversations in the bud.

WRITING FOR THE INTERNET

The Internet is a vast resource that is so full of the written word that somebody somewhere has to be making money doing it. Again, as with business writing, this is a specialist field that tends to be dominated by people working full-time. You are probably better coming up with a site carrying advertising and links to other sites than you are trying to find work writing for other people's sites. That said, if you have a flair for design and find that you are also writing for business (*see* Chapter 11), then maybe designing and writing websites could become a useful sideline business – I know of one playwright who does this.

PHOTOGRAPHY

The ability to take a half-decent photograph is arguably the most useful skill a freelance writer can develop. If you are already a capable photographer, then you might even think of the writing as backing up the photography. Whilst the big-selling magazines can easily afford to hire both specialist writers and photographers, the majority of magazines with a lower circulation cannot. They are often reliant on the writer of an article to provide their pictures as well. If you can offer an editor a words-and-picture package, you are in a far stronger position than someone who can't.

Now, this doesn't mean that you suddenly have to be able to take photographs that are good enough to adorn the front cover of *National Geographic* or *Vogue*. However, it does mean that if you can take a presentable, clear image that relates to your subject matter, then you are making your work far more saleable. An article about cheese-making, with a few sharply focused pictures of the process is obviously far more saleable than one without. If you don't take your own pictures, then you will simply have to split the fee, which may not be over-generous in the first place.

Photography is at a crossroads. Newspaper photographers have been using digital technology for some years and magazines have followed suit. Old-fashioned negative and slide film, which used to be the material of choice for magazines, is now rapidly disappearing. Digital photography has also brought with it a new vocabulary. Megapixels, storage media, TIFF, JPEG and CompactFlash will not necessarily mean anything to everybody reading this. Don't worry too much about it. There is not enough space here to go into detail: if you're interested, buy a handful of digital camera magazines and get a straightforward book from the library.

Your best bet is an SLR camera. SLR stands for Single Lens Reflex and refers to the system it uses for getting light through the lens to the film (whether real or digital). At the time of writing, whilst these have dropped considerably in price, they still represent a hefty investment and the second-hand market isn't flooded with them, although you can pick up some real bargains with film-based cameras. If you do use old-fashioned film, the rule is slides (transparencies) for colour pictures and prints for black and white.

SLRs generally come with interchangeable lenses. This means that you can take both close-up shots from inches away, as well as zooming in on Flintoff's bat as he hoists another one into the pavilion, simply by swapping lenses. Of course, buying all these lenses is also expensive, although canny purchasers will know which 'non-digital' lenses will fit which digital cameras, thereby saving a fortune. It is also likely that you can, at least to begin with, get away with the lens that comes with the camera.

You could, however, be racking up some huge expense without knowing if you will reap any benefit. A second choice would be to buy what is referred to as a 'prosumer' digital camera. This is a halfway house between the kind of camera a family might take on holiday and something a professional would use. They are often neat, compact, well built, lightweight and have built-in zoom lenses. All the big names in the camera world produce decent quality SLRs and prosumer cameras. However, if you are taking pictures that involve movement, such as sports pictures, you won't get away with anything less than a SLR.

Whatever you choose, you must bear in mind the number of pixels the camera offers. Pixels are the small dots that go to make up a picture – perhaps this is at its most obvious when you look at newsprint. What you buy must have at least five *effective* Megapixels. Disregard the number of interpolated pixels, that's a way of altering the number of dots in the picture digitally – they're not the real McCoy. Whilst pundits say that the quality of digital pictures is still not up to that of transparency (slide) film, the likelihood is that it is of good enough standard for you.

Digital photography also has several advantages over its elder sibling. Simple 'doctoring' of pictures is straightforward. Most digital cameras come supplied with basic software that enables you to download pictures onto the computer and then play with them. Whilst magazines don't like you to mess about with the format of a picture too much, you can do simple tasks such as cropping the 'boring' bits of pictures or changing your subject's red eyes, thereby greatly improving your end result.

Perhaps more importantly, for someone hoping to sell variations on an article, or at least to re-use a picture, you don't have to wait for one magazine to get your pictures back to you before you move on to the next. Digital photographs can simply be stored on a computer and you can then copy over exactly the pictures you want onto disk.

Many colleges run courses in photography. If you are a beginner and feel hesitant about it, then taking a course may be the best way for you to learn. Don't forget to ask round friends with an interest; someone who has recently learned how to do something can often explain things to a beginner more clearly than experts who have long since forgotten how difficult it was at the start.

Photography Tips

Tell It Like It Is. In the same way as you need to know what an article is about, you need to be able to tell what story a picture is trying to tell. This may sound obvious, but I once photographed Wastwater in such a way that it looked like a pointillist painting – great for hanging in the hall, lousy for a magazine.

Fill the Frame. Make sure that whatever you are photographing is the obvious subject of the picture. If you want a photograph of the famous knocker on the door of Durham Cathedral, then photograph the knocker and not the whole door. If you are working with digital film, you can always crop what you have done.

Take a Few Shots of Each Subject. It is easy to end up with a blurred photo or have a cloud pass over just as you want to take the picture. People often squint or blink or look away the instant you snap a picture.

Don't Be Too Economical with Film. If you're in Egypt and you mess up a photo, it's not too easy to go back – far cheaper to spend an extra few quid on an additional roll of film. If you are using a digital camera, then it makes little odds how many pictures you take as your 'film' – whatever storage card your camera uses – is reusable.

Avoid the Obvious Clichés. Sunsets are notoriously difficult to photograph and editors are inundated with them.

Take Your Pictures Outdoors Whenever Possible. The light is normally far better outside than it is indoors.

Try Not to Take Pictures in the Middle of the Day. The sun is at its highest and you can end up with some harsh shadows. Early morning and later in the afternoon are best.

Target Your Pictures. For example, a travel article for a camping magazine needs relevant pictures of campsites, tents and happy campers. Cycling magazines want to see cyclists.

For Travel Pieces, Obtain the Local Tourist Leaflet. See where the photographer stood to take his or her picture and take your photos from there as well. This will enable you to get some good basic shots.

Use a Tripod If You Can. This will steady the camera and reduce the likelihood of blurring. If you can't use a tripod, lean on walls, your companion, the backs of chairs or simply hold the camera in such a way that you have one hand supporting the camera body and the other working the buttons.

Get People in Your Pictures. Landscapes, pictures of buildings and street scenes often look far better if there is someone in them.

Avoid Description. If the photo tells the story, don't repeat it in print.

Look for Bright Colours. Get some vibrant colours in your pictures – red always seems to work particularly well.

Look at Photos in Magazines and Newspapers. Ask yourself what you like or dislike about a certain photo and then either avoid or imitate.

Experiment. Try to develop an eye for the unusual; 'same but different' is as good a rule of thumb for supplying pictures as it is for articles to magazines.

Start Your Own Small-Scale Photographic Library. Don't keep every picture you have ever taken – throw out the dross. I cull mine from time to time and keep the better transparencies in plastic wallets in ring binders and keep digital pictures on backup disks.

Use Pictures to Trigger Ideas. Sorting your collection on a wet winter evening means you can see if there are any pictures that give you an idea for an article. You may have to go back and update them, but it is one way of keeping your mind alert to new possibilities.

Photograph People Doing Things. If you are writing a feature on a blacksmith, make sure that you photograph them at work. If they are shoeing a horse then you can get a picture of a person and an animal, and editors love that. Don't get your subject to turn round and smile at the camera, but try to capture them mid-activity.

Be Kind to Your Subjects. If you're photographing someone of generous proportions, you can make them look slimmer by sitting them down and hiding their bottom with a cushion.

Think of Other Ways of Photographing Objects. When a professional photographer came to interview me about my book *Escape from the Rat Race*, instead of simply photographing the book he grouped a computer mouse, telephone, portable phone and pager around the book to illustrate that it was a bit of an antidote to the technological pressures of modern life. Look for ideas like that. After all, you've got the imagination to write, so you must have the imagination to make visual leaps as well.

Practise. Yes, it's obvious, but take your camera out and about and take pictures wherever you can. Think what shots you might take if you were working for a particular magazine. The more pictures you take, the better your chances of success.

Permission. You need permission from people if they can be clearly identified from one of your pictures.

Exercise: Photography

Take a camera out onto the streets of your town or village. Look up at the buildings: see if there is anything of interest to photograph high up. Watch what people do and photograph them. Is there any wildlife? What would you photograph for your town brochure?

---

11 WRITING FOR BUSINESS

Most of the very large companies employ Public Relations specialists, whose role it is to promote the company's activities in the press and other media. There is probably little point in trying to market your services to these companies, although I have heard of authors who have been paid handsomely to produce company histories for larger concerns. The places where you might find you can sell your services are amongst smaller businesses, voluntary groups and organizations in the public sector.

Writing for business has its own set of skills. If you haven't done any of this kind of work before, it would be extremely hard to convince someone that you are capable of so doing. It's the catch-22 of all work – if you can't prove that you can do it then why should anyone hire you, and until someone hires you, you can't prove that you can do it.

You need to be able to show a prospective client some work. If you haven't done any writing for business, there are straightforward ways in which you can build up a small portfolio of work. First, contact local charity organizations or your local Council for Voluntary Services and explain to them that you are available to write press releases and other promotional material. Be careful not to overdo it; charities are often thankful for help and some are a little too quick to give a volunteer more than they can manage. It is one way of learning your trade.

Second, use any local contacts you have. Say, for instance, that you have a friend, Charlie, who owns a garage specializing in car repairs. You could offer to write promotional material for your friend, explaining exactly why you want to do it. Be honest and tell Charlie that you don't expect any payment, but that you are trying to develop some work in this field and need to build up some experience. If you don't have a friend like Charlie, then try friends of friends, or just ask a local shop with whom you've done business if you can use them as a guinea pig. The difficulty here is that sometimes people wonder what the catch will be if they are getting something for nothing.

Once you have a small portfolio of clients, you can then approach other businesses. Put together a letter in which you:

- Introduce yourself.
- Explain what service you can offer the potential client.

- Explain why your service is important – what benefits will it bring the client?
- Enclose some samples of your work.

If you can't write the kind of letter that will promote yourself in this way, then writing for business is not for you. Writing for business is, in the main, concerned with promotion. Although many of us find it far easier to sing other people's praises than our own, I would suggest that if you can't sell yourself to businesses, then you can't write what businesses need. Don't feel depressed by this. Not all of us can do everything; we are not all built the same way. Writing for business is tough, demanding and, frankly, often tedious.

What Does Business Want?

Advertisements

There are several types of common advertisements that you can help to write. Forget the fancier end of advertising, where everyone is trying to dream up the next great slogan; there are more workaday advertisements that can be written. These can include advertising for personnel and promoting a company's goods or services.

It would seem that writing a job advert is pure common sense, but you would be astounded at the number of adverts that fail to say what the job is about or even leave out contact details. A job advert can be as simple as this:

> Busy city-centre pub seeks part-time bar staff for weekend work. Prior experience of bar work an advantage. Please send CV to The Red Lion, The Avenue, Scuttleborough, ZF23 2RT. For an informal chat about the work, phone Barbara on 001100 88888.

A well-written job advert should include:

- A job title, with a brief explanation including something about the organization if necessary.
- A brief outline of the previous experience required.
- How you can apply – whether by CV or application form, for example.
- Where to apply.
- If there is anyone who can be contacted for further information.
- The closing date.

On the other hand, writing a sales advert is possibly a little trickier. The corny expression is 'sell the sizzle, not the steak'. This means that you need to persuade the reader of the benefits of the product. So what if the car tyres grip the road better? Tell the reader that the tyres are safer. Customers want to know that they are getting a good deal or great service or a better product. They want to know how what you sell them is going to improve their lives.

There are also other forms of product advertising that aren't simply notices in the newspaper.

Promotional Material

The chances are that some kind of promotional materials drops through your letterbox every week. Some of it will be direct mail from companies from whom you have bought something in the past, offering something else you might want. Some will be entirely speculative, unaddressed material, offering double glazing or new soffits and fascias or electric garage doors. Many companies' catalogues are produced on a three- or six-monthly basis and are read with interest by people who buy regularly from them.

Writing this kind of material is far more difficult than it might at first look. You need to be able to get your message across in the first few words, and we all know that the fewer words you have to play with, the harder it is. Your text also has to be readable by anyone. It must be snappy, direct and attention-grabbing. As with all work of this sort, it is well worth reading aloud what you have written. You also need to talk directly to the customer: 'Do you want your car to shine?'

If you want to drum up business, why not take any badly written promotional material that has come through your door, contact the company that sent it and suggest (politely) ways in which it could be improved.

Press Releases

If you have ever wondered how the newspapers know that your local supermarket has just served its millionth customer or that your pizza takeaway is branching out into curries or, for that matter, that a local author has just published a new book, then welcome to the world of the press release. A press release is a device used by companies and other organizations to get information to the public, without having to pay for advertising, which can cost hundreds or thousands of pounds. This is likely to be your best area for business writing.

Press releases are a powerful tool for business, because people are far more likely to believe what they read in an editorial than they are in an advertisement. However, editors are aware that they are essentially giving free space in their newspapers and magazines and that they have to tread carefully. They are, therefore, looking for press releases that provide them with stories. The fact that the supermarket has served another customer *is not* a story; the fact that it's their one millionth customer *is*. This means that if you are asked to write a press release, you need to be looking for a story, preferably one with a human (or animal) interest.

As with feature articles, most people don't want to read about objects or things, they want to read about other people. If you are writing a press release for a company that has just invented a little device that enables you to open those little plastic pots of milk without the contents flying across the table, then it could make a good story. Despite the fact that this is a much-needed gadget, it is not half as good a story as writing about the person or the team that invented it – how they came up with the idea, how they developed it, and where they are going with the idea in the future.

'Bert Smith is a Writer' is not a story, it is an advertisement. 'It's Bert Smith's Tenth Book in as Many Years' is a story. 'It's Bert Smith's Tenth Book in Ten Years, Despite the Fact that He's Dyslexic' is a good story.

If you are going to try to write press releases, it is worth taking a few minutes out to think about how you read a newspaper. Few people actually plough through a newspaper from one end to the other. We skim through, and when a headline or a picture catches our eyes, we swoop in and read. Often, we only read the first few lines. We don't read newspapers in the same way as we read a novel, for instance, where we might be prepared to linger and savour. We read newspapers in front of the telly, on the bus, in the loo, on a coffee break. Often, whilst we are reading the paper, we are also involved in something else.

Remember that news items are always cut from the bottom. Make sure that your most important information is contained in the first couple of paragraphs, otherwise you might not get any editorial space at all. If your press release is about Bert's achievement, stick to the main point. We probably don't want to read about all the other books he's written – that would look like a shopping list. However, we are almost certainly going to want to know what his most recent book is, what it's about, where we can buy it, how much it costs and the canny writer of a press release can slip this in under the reader's radar.

You can see from this that even if you never intend writing press releases for other people, writing them for yourself can be handy. Small publishers are often stretched when it comes to publicizing books. A well-written press release to your local paper or a relevant publication can reap dividends. I have even had commissions for articles off the back of press releases about books. To sum up:

- Get a catchy title.
- Write about the inventor, not the invention – people want to read about people.
- Look for a hook to your story – it must stick in the reader's mind.
- Think specifically – we want an actual story, not general waffle.
- Don't send out an advertisement – it won't get printed.
- Get your most interesting information in early.
- Build up some information about the person involved in your press release and then quote them.
- Get a good, strong picture that will interest the readers.

You then need to target your press release to specific journalists. Find out their names, spell their names correctly, get their titles right and don't forget to include on your press release such basic information as the date of the press release (or the date it is embargoed till) and the contact person for further information.

Press release

**Sid's Tiles, The Avenue, Scuttleborough, ZF23 2RT
Press Release – For Immediate Release**

Sid's Tiles Go Dutch

Local tile manufacturer, Sid Thistledown, has launched not one, but two branches of his DIY store Sid's Tiles in mainland Europe.

'I've been wanting to expand onto the continent for some time now,' says Sid, founder and owner of Sid's Tiles, which already has forty-seven outlets in the UK. 'The sudden surge of interest in DIY in Holland has meant that the time is right.'

Sid's expansion is not only good news for the citizens of Amsterdam and Rotterdam, but also for locals in Anytown, headquarters of Sid's Tiles.

'Not only will we be taking on more staff in Holland, but we'll also be taking on more warehouse staff here,' says Sid.

For further information, contact Harry Manager on 00 11 00 44 88 77.

Newsletters

These are a common way for organizations to let their staff or customers know what's going on. They are often produced on a regular basis and range in quality from a couple of sides of A4 paper to glossy magazines. Although many are written in-house, there may occasionally be openings for a freelancer to work either as an editor or writer. I recently noticed an advertisement for someone to do precisely this for a college on a one-day-a-week basis. A job like that could provide a good, steady income, whilst allowing the writer time to follow other pursuits.

Writing a newsletter can be a time-consuming business, though. That one day a week may look tempting, but it might mean working a day's worth of hours over the entire week, so that you find yourself covering events at all times of the day or evening and at weekends.

Management Reports

It is rare for a freelance writer to be asked to write a report for a company. Perhaps occasionally a company might want to put information together in a way that has a more general appeal than a typical management report, with its wooden prose, passive verbs and convoluted, mangled English. If you have to write one, there is a tightrope to walk. That convoluted, mangled English makes a lot of managers believe that they are far more intelligent than they are; it becomes the language they expect to see in a management report and it is hard to change that. 'Intensive and extensive discussions took place concerning the introduction of a bespoke air-conditioning system before its eventual commission was decided upon' is appalling, flatulent English. Changing it to 'we decided to buy an air-conditioning system' is neater, but that may not be what they want to see. Whoever pays the piper calls the tune.

Company Histories

Occasionally, companies will commission writers to produce a history of the company. This often seems to be the case with businesses that are still under the control of the people who created the business. This is a potentially lucrative market as you are being paid to tell the world what a wonderful chap Sid Thistledown, the founder and director of Thistledown Mouldings is. The resulting book is often then filled with glossy pictures and given away to important clients and senior staff.

Your biggest difficulty here is in agreeing a fee. If the company has good archives and other records and you are allowed free access, then it makes the work easier. You will also need to interview people, often at length and in depth. Indeed, the research element of the book may take far longer than the writing. You need to weigh up how long it will take and agree a fee for the entire project, preferably in staged payments – for instance first payment on commission, second payment on first draft (which will have to be approved by Sid Thistledown) and third payment on final delivery. You might also try to work into the project expenses payments and have these reimbursed on a regular basis. It is vital to agree a timescale. If in doubt, contact the Society of Authors for guidance.

Another String to the Bow

It is highly unlikely that you would find work as a freelance advertising copy-writer, coming up with nifty slogans to help shift products, but as we have seen there is no reason why you shouldn't put your writing skills to use in helping to promote businesses and other organizations or to help them with their internal communications.

To enter the world of PR and marketing, you would need to build up a lot of contacts. Whilst it may be that this would suit you admirably as a career, I would suspect that as you are reading a book about writing non-fiction, you probably have slightly different ambitions. If your aim is to be producing published articles and books, then seguing into the world of promotional and business writing could deflect you from that goal. On the other hand, being asked to do the occasional piece of writing for business can be a useful and lucrative adjunct to your main work. At the worst, it gets your name out there.

12 Getting and Staying Organized

Writers are not necessarily the first people you would turn to if you needed to get yourself organized. Their offices and studies tend to be littered with piles of paper, their accounts months out of date, their workspace cluttered and untidy. It is almost as though being organized might kill off the creativity that allows a writer to think, develop ideas and tinker with projects.

Whilst this might be true of a Nobel Laureate, I am unconvinced that the same is true of the jobbing author. In fact, I would suggest that a jobbing author, who probably has to have a dozen projects on the go at any one time must be extremely well organized purely to stay solvent. Being well organized doesn't mean crushing the creativity out of you. It simply means that when someone telephones you about a job you are doing for them, you can dig out the relevant folder, tell them of your progress and keep your customer happy. After all, you are running a business.

Creating a Workspace

Working from home is many people's ideal. Your travel-to-work time is negligible and, if you put your head down, you can produce a day's output in the same time as a suburban commuter spends simply getting to and from work.

If you are going to write, it is vital that you have somewhere you can work in relative peace. The ideal is to have a study or office that is dedicated to your writing; when you are in that room, that is what you are doing. Whilst you are working, you can close the door as a signal to family to keep out. When you finish work, you can close the door so as to separate your work from your home life.

You may not be that lucky. Your best option is if you can dedicate a room to your work, but we have to be realistic. It would take years to earn enough to pay to move to a larger house. The dining room or a table in the spare room may be absolutely fine to begin with, but not everyone has the luxury of even that much space. You might find yourself working in the corner of your sitting room or bedroom, or even bed-sitting room. If you can, try to make a corner of a room into a genuine office space. Nowadays, you can buy smart furniture that means that your computer can be shut away in a cupboard that opens out to become a little office, with pull-out work surfaces and shelves.

If you can use the spare room, do so. Decide how often anyone actually uses it. If the truth is that it isn't occupied a great deal, you might be able to get away with creating a dual-purpose room with a bed-settee, or transform it into a study and get round the spare bed problem with one of the latest, extraordinarily comfortable air beds that can be stored almost anywhere, inflate to a bed-type height and can be moved into the room when needed. You will lose your office when you have visitors, but it's often difficult to get on with any work when you have guests anyway.

Another alternative is the good old garden shed. If you are handy and have a large enough garden, you can create an excellent workspace in a shed and even insulate it against the worst of the effects of the weather and run electricity to it, all for a few hundred pounds. Britain has a long history of shed-based writers – Roald Dahl and Philip Pullman are just two who have plied their trade from the bottom of the garden. It is certainly a far cheaper alternative to buying a larger house.

Whatever you decide, do try to treat that space as a working space. If you don't have a professional attitude towards your working space, you are going to find it hard to get a professional attitude towards your work in general.

CREATING A WORKING ENVIRONMENT

As well as creating a suitable workspace, you may like to consider trying to create the right environment in which to work. The American author Stephen King manages to write his novels whilst heavy metal rock music rips from big speakers. James Herriot famously wrote his best-selling vet books in the sitting room, with the TV set blaring, whilst all of family life flowed around him. Not all of us could cope with that; some people have to work in absolute silence.

As with anything that helps you to write, you need to develop your own strategy. Find out what works for you and use it. However, some of the various techniques that authors use include:

- Playing baroque music at low volume – good for covering the silence when the keyboard isn't clattering, and you don't find yourself singing along to any lyrics.
- Burning aromatherapy candles – I'm not convinced by the pseudo-science behind them, but if they give your nose a clue that it is time to get on with some work, they can't be entirely useless.
- Keeping a flask of iced water handy – coffee and tea are fine, but you can find yourself drinking far too much than is good for you. Iced water with a slice of lemon is a way of cutting down on the caffeine intake, and means that you can sip away to your heart's content.

- Keeping a scrap pad handy on the desk. Whenever you are working on one piece ideas come to you about others. Jot them down on the scrap pad or use a dictation machine to record them quickly, rather than interrupting your flow.
- Ignoring the telephone. Using an answering machine is perfectly acceptable. Breaking off to answer the telephone often puts the curse on a writing session and it is hard to get back into the flow. A ringing phone is hard to ignore, but try to let it go to the answerphone.

Tools of the Trade

One of the great aspects of being a freelance writer (even if only in your spare time) is that you can get away with having to buy very little equipment indeed. In theory, you could probably do all your writing for free on the computer in the local library, save it onto disk, print it out at a friend's house for the price of a pint and with a couple of envelopes and a book of stamps you're in business. However, although I suspect there might be one or two folk who get away with this, you are probably much better off trying to set up at home in the space you have dedicated to the job.

Handwriting your work is fine when you are working in rough or for your first draft. It is completely unacceptable for anything you want to send to an editor. The least you need to be able to use is a typewriter, but even then you could be placing yourself at a disadvantage. Computers are here to stay. Any advice I can give about which model to buy will be out of date before I write the next chapter, let alone by the time this book is printed, so I will limit myself to a few general observations.

A laptop has the huge advantage of being portable, so you can work almost anywhere, and they are increasingly cheap. This is especially useful if you can't devote a space in your house exclusively to your work. Many writers start out on the dining room table, so a laptop is handy to be able to clear away easily. They are also good for working in libraries, cafés or even on trains, many of which now have electrical sockets just for that purpose.

However, if you do have space for a desktop computer so much the better, and you are likely to get a more powerful machine for your money. Buy a good-sized screen. If you are going to be staring at it for long stretches of time it is useful to have a decent size of monitor as this helps to cut down on eye strain. Besides, if you want to work in cafés, libraries and trains, then you can always buy a pad of paper at a fraction of the price.

Software

You will, of course, need software to run on your computer. It is probably best to go for one of the most common word-processing packages as these can be read by most computers. However, if you know what you are doing you can buy extraordinarily inexpensive software that does just about everything its more expensive, more readily available brothers do, but at a fraction of the cost. In fact, the software I used to type this book was completely free. It's not stolen either! It is called Open Office and is available free of charge from the Sun Microsystems website (*see* Appendix). You do need to know how to save your work in a format that is acceptable to editors, which usually means either Text files or Word files. Open Office, for instance, allows me to save all my documents as though they were Microsoft Word files or in RTF (rich text format), meaning my work can normally be read by other computers.

Another useful piece of software is an accounts package. You can write your own spreadsheets for the purpose (using free software), but home accounts software packages are so cheap, you might be tempted to buy one. Microsoft often sells packages of programs that include word-processing software (such as Works or Windows) and a home accounts program.

If you have physical difficulties or are a real non-typist, then you can even dictate your work directly into your computer using voice recognition software. Alternatively, you can use a typing service. Provided your handwriting is neat enough for somebody to read, you will be able to find someone who will do this for you. You may even find someone who can still take dictation. If you put an advert in your local supermarket, you might find someone looking to earn some extra income from home. Magazines such as *The Author* often have advertisements from people offering secretarial services. As well as providing you with your work on paper, laid out to your specification, these services should also be able to provide you with a computer disk of your work.

I maintain that even if you are the world's slowest typist, it is best to be able to type your own work. If you prefer handwriting in the first instance, then fine. Typing up your work gives you a chance to make alterations as you go. However, having your work on a computer means that it is extremely easy to make minor alterations, to print out copies as and when needed and to present it professionally without having to rely on anyone else's help.

PRINTER

I would suggest that as a writer the most important part of your home computer set-up is your printer. If you can afford the few extra pounds to buy a laser printer, do so. Once you have got over the initial cost they are far cheaper to run than inkjets, you smudge the end product less often and they tend to give a more professional look to your work.

A laser printer is also a much more economical buy in the long-term and it is possible to adjust the print quality on a laser printer so that it uses less toner – the powder that sticks to the page to form the print. I always have mine on the lowest setting. No one has ever quibbled about the print quality and I reckon I can get around double the life out of a cartridge this way. A further way to expand cartridge life is to use a cartridge-refilling service. You can even do it yourself, provided you know how to take the cartridge apart (this is

> ### A Basic Home Office for a Writer
>
> - Desk or table, preferably a big one (L-shaped are fantastic).
> - Good-quality chair – preferably one with a high back and arms. Go for a 'manager's chair', rather than a 'typist's chair'. Test before you buy.
> - Storage that will keep your stationery dry, flat and wrinkle-free.
> - Filing cabinet.
> - Computer with Internet access and the biggest screen you can get away with.
> - Printer – laser is best.
> - Scanner – you can use the scanner and printer together as a substitute for a photocopier.
> - Telephone and answering machine – use one with your own voice on it, it is so much friendlier than an electronic voice.
> - Dictation machine – handy for taking down quick ideas that you have when you're halfway through something else.

normally the hardest part of the refilling process). You can buy laser printers that have a built-in scanner. This means that you can copy pictures into your computer, but more usefully, it also means that the printer can double as a photocopier, normally without having to switch on the computer.

THE INTERNET

A few years ago, every business needed a fax machine. Nowadays, an email address is a must-have. It is probably impossible to function as a writer without the Internet. Not only does it give you access to almost instant correspondence via email, but the resources that are at your disposal via the World Wide Web are enormous. The Web is also a necessity for any kind of research (*see* Chapter 5). Broadband is more expensive, but the advantages in terms of speed easily make up for the additional cost. Don't forget that if you do use the Internet, you need anti-virus software. An infected games computer is annoying; an infected work machine potentially puts your livelihood up the spout.

STATIONERY

It is easy to go to town on stationery if you're not too careful. Nowadays, you can pick up decent quality white A4 paper almost anywhere. Even supermarkets sell it by the ream (500 sheets). If you use an inkjet printer, you may find that you have to buy slightly more expensive paper otherwise the ink will either smudge on the surface or soak into the paper too much (it's another good reason for buying a laser printer). The usual 80gsm paper will do. Slightly pricier, but kinder to the world in which we live is recycled paper.

Decent envelopes are a must. I'm as keen as anyone else to do my bit for recycling, but I always send my copy out (when not sending it electronically) in a smart new envelope. I tend to buy five different sorts of envelope: big ones that will fit anything; C4, which takes A4-size paper without the need for folding; C5, which takes A4 folded in half (A5-size); and two sorts of white DL envelopes (with and without windows). Window envelopes are so much easier to use as you have to type the address on the letter anyway. I recycle envelopes within my office, using them to store papers and so forth, rather than sending them out, as I don't want my editors receiving anything too scruffy from me.

Headed Paper

You don't need to go to the expense of headed notepaper. It is simple enough to create a computerized template with your name, address, email address and phone number. It is up to you if you want to describe yourself as a freelance writer; I don't, on the basis that what I do should be obvious from the content of the letter. Avoid fancy fonts and logos, though – they tend to look silly or pretentious, or both. If you have a colour printer, then you can use it for your heading, but it is probably best not to do much more than that. It is also useful to create some 'With compliments' slips that you can simply include with anything that doesn't need a full-blown covering letter.

Business Cards

Again, you can make these on your computer and print them out on card. They are not always the best quality when you do this, but they are probably adequate. Commercially-produced business cards, which will normally be of a higher standard, can be bought inexpensively. You won't have a great demand for them, so if you are not making any money yet, this is an area on which you can cut down. Your business card should contain all your contact details and the fact that you are a writer. If you want, you can have a little logo, but be circumspect. A naff logo will put people off far more than a good one will attract them.

Basic Stationery Requirements

- Large envelopes.
- Envelopes that take A4 paper without folding (C4 size).
- Medium envelopes that take A4 paper folded in half (C5 size).
- Window envelopes (DL size).
- Plain white envelopes (DL size).
- 80gsm white copying paper.
- A4 notepads.
- Reporters' notebooks.
- A5 and A4 spiral-bound books – excellent for individual projects.

KEEPING A RECORD OF YOUR WORK

When you first start out, it is probably easy to keep tabs on what you're doing. However, as you begin to get busier, you are going to need some kind of system for recording what you do. In addition to the ideas book mentioned in Chapter 1, it is also worth keeping a separate sheet of where you send ideas. I call this my 'pitches sheet'. Every now and then I look to see if I have enough pitches doing the rounds. If I don't, I earmark a few days, possibly even a couple of weeks, during which I will do nothing but write pitches for articles and develop ideas I have had for books into full-blown book proposals.

As the replies come in from pitches, ranging from the 'are you mad? Never darken my door again', to the 'you are a genius, here have a cheque for a million pounds' (actually, that has never happened, but I can always dream), I keep a note of these. I then transfer any successful pitches into my 'work output sheet', more of which anon.

I use two simple spreadsheets on the computer for this process. You could equally well use a couple of sheets of paper. I like using the computer because I can cut and paste from one sheet to the other (I keep them in the same file for convenience) and the spreadsheet has a nifty device that enables you to attach a note to an item. So, for instance, an editor might turn something down, but say that she is happy to consider the idea in eighteen months or so. I can attach a note that tells me this, which is indicated in the relevant 'cell' (square) of the spreadsheet by a little red marker. Every now and then, I read through all the attached notes and take appropriate action.

The first spreadsheet, for any pitches I make, is a simple five-column sheet that gives me basic information. I simply want to know the date I pitched the idea, what the idea was – this can be brief as I can always refer to my ideas book for more information – and who I pitched the idea to (an editor or publisher or local organization). I also make a note of what type of idea it was: a book, an article, a course, a play or whatever and in the last column I record the outcome of the pitch. Normally this last column is filled with a straightforward 'yes' or 'no'. On occasions, you get an editor who likes the idea, but wants you to take a slightly different slant, or wants to think about it and so has sent a holding email, or wants a different version of what you had in mind.

My second sheet is a useful listing of work that I have successfully managed to place that I can then use in several ways. The sheet has just six headings, and again I add any notes as necessary. When I transfer items from my 'pitches sheet' to my 'work output sheet', I initially only complete the items headed 'description', 'purchaser' and if I know the fee (and sometimes you don't know the precise fee, so have to estimate), putting it in the column headed 'expected fee'. I use the first column to record the actual date on which I have sent the finished work to an editor or publisher or taught the workshop and submitted an invoice. This means that any items that do not have a date in front of them are jobs that I still have to do. Printing out undated items gives me a simple to-do list.

It also gives me an idea if I am going to earn enough money. As fees come in in dribs and drabs, knowing that you have work to the value of a few thousand pounds out there in the ether settles your nerves (and those of your bank manager). It also means I can keep tabs on what happens to work that is accepted for publication and whether I need to chase payment or not.

A spreadsheet also enables you to do simple calculations automatically. My spreadsheet automatically gives me the total of the 'Expected fees' column, which gives me an idea of how much I am earning. It does the same for the 'amount received' column, which tells me how much I've earned, although I don't use this for genuine accounting, but as a rough guide (as I also make money from other sources, such as Public Lending Right, royalties on books and so forth). At the end of the year, I can then copy over into fresh spreadsheets any outstanding items – both pitches and work I need to do.

You might think that all this is a bit of a faff. There is no doubt that such a system is overkill if you're only ever penning the occasional piece. If you are trying to make a success as a full-time writer, you will soon see that keeping these kinds of records is a boon. It is much harder to keep tabs on where you've pitched what and who has said 'yes' or 'no' when you've been writing for a year or two. Of course, you'll probably want to adapt these records to suit yourself and you may prefer to keep all this information in a notebook, rather than on the computer. It is important to have some kind of system, though.

Example Pitches Sheet

Date	Idea	Where Pitched	What?	Outcome
1 June 2006	Murder casebook	Murder Press	Book	No
4 June 2006	Camping in Brittany	Backpacker Magazine	Article	Yes
7 June 2006	Writing Non-Fiction for Profit	Writers' College	Course	Try again in November
10 June 2006	Writing Non-Fiction for Profit	Writers' University	Course	Yes, need to speak to Mrs Smith ext. 252 re details
12 June 2006	The Parish Closes of Brittany	I Love Brittany Magazine	Article	Yes
14 June 2006	Murder casebook	Assassin Press	Book	Possible (see note)

Example Work Output Sheet

Date	Description	Purchaser	Expected Fee	Date Published	Amount Received
19 April 2006	Murder on the Towpath	Canal Killer Magazine	£150.00	1 June 2006	£150.00
22 April 2006	Murder in Brittany	Brittany Killer Magazine	£200.00		
24 May 2006	Writing Non-fiction for Profit	One-day Workshops Ltd	£150.00		
	Murder on the Towpath in Brittany	Brittany Canal Killer Magazine			

GETTING PAID

A large number of magazines pay on publication. To an extent, you can understand their point of view; they can stockpile articles and then smooth their cash flow by paying for them when they use them. Many of these magazines are not wealthy outfits, although you will hear the same excuse trotted out by magazine companies that are PLCs. If you look at it from a different perspective though, it is not a fair way to do business. Imagine walking into a clothes shop in July, taking a pullover and then informing the staff that it's a Christmas present and you will pay for it when the recipient eventually wears it. This is essentially what these magazines are doing to you.

Magazines should pay on delivery or acceptance. The reality is that many don't. It shouldn't be unreasonable however, for them to agree that you should be paid either on publication, or within three months, whichever is sooner. Some magazines will argue that, as they pay by the page, they don't know how much they should pay you. After all, if your item stretches to four pages rather than the three it might normally make, it's to your benefit. It is worth making sure that you know what you are to be paid, even if that amount is flexible. I recently signed a deal for an article-and-pictures package that promised me a certain rate per page and that the article would be four to six pages, so at least I know where I stand.

The National Union of Journalists is opposed to payment on publication, although many writers allow it simply in order to make their lives easier. Whatever payment date you agree on, there is no excuse for late payment. If someone owes you money, don't make excuses on their behalf; send them a reminder invoice. Also make sure that your invoices not only carry the words

'Terms 30 days nett', but the following sentence: '*We understand and will exercise our statutory right to claim interest and compensation for debt recovery costs under the late payment legislation if we are not paid according to agreed credit terms*'. If a publisher fails to pay after an invoice and a reminder, you are fully entitled to not only charge a penalty payment, but also to charge interest at 8 per cent above the basic rate.

Often, by sending your new, larger invoice you will simply frighten the initial payment out of the publisher. You might want to settle for that or you might want to pursue the matter further. If you still don't receive any payment, you need to send a further statement of what is now owed (plus even more interest) by some form of postage that needs to be signed for at their end, together with the information that if this is not paid within fourteen days, you will take the matter to the Small Claims Court. If they don't pay, stick to your guns and take them to court. It may be hassle, but it's only fair – you did the work and you have not been paid. Essentially, they have stolen from you. If they are doing it to you, they are probably doing it to others.

One of my writing students, hearing that I was involved in a tussle to get money from a magazine (they have since paid), said 'You don't want to make too much of a fuss, they won't take anything from you again.' She was right. They won't be taking anything from me again because I am tired of having to send three invoices just to get my money. Someone else can have the dubious pleasure of supplying them with copy. Luckily, even if some magazines are sluggish, few are downright dishonest. The likelihood is that you will be paid ... eventually.

What Will a Publisher Pay for a Book?

With publication deals for books, the situation is a little more complex. The good news is that if you are offered a book deal, you are entitled to membership of the Society of Authors. The SoA is an excellent organization (*see* Appendix for details), which offers writers many useful services. Most importantly, they have a contract-vetting service.

Most publishers will pay you what is termed an 'advance', which is more precisely an advance on future royalties. This means that they are prepared to gamble a certain sum of money against the number of copies they think the book will sell and pay you some proportion of your share of those profits upfront. It is often payable in stages and typically you will receive half on signing the contract and half on delivery of the manuscript, although some publishers may divide your advance into thirds (payable on signature, delivery of manuscript and publication). Occasionally, you will receive one payment on delivery of the manuscript.

Publishers obviously want to get the best deal they can and so should you. You can negotiate, although it is unrealistic of you to think that a book that is likely to sell only a few thousand copies should get a six-figure advance. It isn't always the advance that is important. If the book suddenly takes off and sells many more copies than everyone expected, you will receive further payments.

Unless your advance was disproportionately high, you should receive further royalty payments, once your book has 'earned' its advance. Publishers usually pay royalties on a yearly or twice-yearly basis. It is also possible that your book might be sold to an overseas market, which can bring in additional income, as can registering your book for Public Lending Rights and with the Authors' Licensing and Collecting Society (*see* Appendix).

Most publishers will provide you with a handful of copies of your book, which you usually end up giving out to family and friends. They normally allow you to buy your book at the wholesale rate. Unless there is a clause that forbids it – and most publishers are happy to strike out such a clause anyway – you can then sell copies of your book for a small profit, although it does mean that you always need to carry a small stock of them. Don't expect to make a fortune from this, but it can be a handy way of making a bit of extra income.

KEEPING ACCOUNTS AND PAYING TAX

If it is useful to keep records for yourself, it is vital when it comes to keeping them for the taxman. As soon as you start earning any money from your work, the tax office is going to want to know. Many larger companies have to inform the tax office who they have paid as freelancers during the previous tax year, so you're unlikely to get away with pretending that you have never had the money, should the thought have even crossed your mind.

This section is no more than a vague outline of the tax situation for writers; I am far from an expert in these matters, the rules often change and there is no substitute for professional advice. A professional accountant, certainly one who specializes in writers' affairs, will be able to give you much more precise information and advice. Furthermore, if you aren't resident in the United Kingdom, different rules will almost certainly apply.

However, if you are UK-resident and are making money from your writing, you will need to declare the fact on your income tax return form. For a start, it is illegal not to declare earnings and, given that many publishing companies make declarations to the tax office about whom they've paid, you would be unlikely to get away with it for long.

The taxman defines a professional writer as someone who writes regularly with the intention of making a profit or who is gathering material or researching or preparing for publication. In theory, then, you could tell the taxman that you are 'preparing to write' and try to claim tax relief on all your expenditure. In this case, if your expenditure exceeds income, your losses can be offset against other tax liabilities, although some tax offices might argue that they will offset the loss against future earnings from writing. You are unlikely to get away with playing at writing. You must have some serious intentions, otherwise your tax office will eventually come down on you. Occasional small bits of income are not considered proof that you are carrying out a trade.

However, all is not lost. There are special rules that govern new businesses or professions in their first few years of operation, so you need to check the latest details of these. Furthermore, if you keep full records of the work you are doing – speculative articles, book proposals and that kind of thing – you stand a better chance of proving that you are a writer, even if not yet successful. It is vital to keep accurate records of income and expenditure. You can get lots of useful information from your local tax office or online.

What Counts as Income?

Any money you get from anywhere in the world that relates to your writing counts as income. This will include advances on royalties (money paid in advance for a future book), royalties (money paid for books that are still selling), money for any commissions you might have had, the sale of articles and copyright, and any reimbursed expenses that you have had. If you have done any freelance lecturing or teaching, this should also be included (although don't include payments where tax is deducted at source). If you sell your own books, this also counts as income. Prizes and grants are a bit of a grey area. Generally, prizes and awards aren't taxable, although some Arts Council grants may be. If in doubt, why not ask the people who have given you the award?

What Counts as Expenditure?

You can claim for all of the following, provided that the expenditure has been incurred as part of the running of your business – that of being a writer:

Office Expenses. This includes the telephone, fax machine, computer software, Internet, postage, stationery, printing, insurance, small items of equipment, and cost of heating and lighting (or a proportion if it is your own home).

Transport Costs. Including the use of cars (including your own), taxis, trains, planes or buses. For your own car, you might find it simplest to charge the mileage costs to your business. The cost per mile is usually based on engine size. You can find out the relevant mileage costs by contacting the tax office. Keep a record of your business mileage.

Subscriptions to Societies. If you belong to the Society of Authors or the National Union of Journalists, for instance, such subscriptions can also be offset against tax.

Professional Services. Accountants' and lawyers' fees as well as any payments you make to researchers, proofreaders or typists are considered tax-deductible.

Books and the Like. You can also set the cost of books and periodicals needed for your work against tax.

Rent and Rates. You can, in theory, offset a proportion of your council tax and your water rates against tax. However, that could lead you into a tricky situation whereby you might be expected to pay a proportion of the capital gains on part of your house when you come to re-sell. Professional advice is needed on this issue.

Capital Equipment. You can also offset the cost of buying larger pieces of equipment, although this is often spread over a number of years. It used to be the accepted practice that capital equipment depreciated at 25 per cent per year: so if you paid £1,000 for a desk, then you could offset £250 in the year you bought it, then in the second year 25 per cent of the remaining value of £750 (£187.50) and so on. However, as so much modern technology is outmoded the moment you get it back from the shop, different rules apply, depending on what you buy. Check with your tax office or, if you're using an accountant, let them do the work for you.

VAT

You don't have to register for VAT until your turnover exceeds a certain amount, which changes annually, so you need to check the latest threshold. You'd have to be doing extremely well as a non-fiction author to register, so it is unlikely. You can, however, register on a voluntary basis if you think it is worth recouping the VAT you pay out.

Saving for Tax

When you do start making a little bit of money, it is not a bad idea to put some aside for tax. If you are self-employed, you have to pay your tax in two lump sums every six months, together with any additional National Insurance you might owe. The figure for each tax year is an estimate based on your earnings in the previous tax year, so if you have a particularly good year, you might find yourself paying out heavily the following year when times aren't so good.

You can open a high-interest savings account with just a few pounds. It is not a bad idea to have a system whereby you automatically put 30 per cent of any gross income into such an account. If your tax bill is for less than you've saved, then you have still got money in the pot for next year. Besides, it'll provide you with a kitty for a rainy day and, if you don't have a company pension, you are going to have to think about some way of saving for your old age.

National Insurance

If you are self-employed, you will also have to pay self-employed National Insurance. You have to pay a weekly amount, which is normally paid on a quarterly basis but can also be paid by monthly direct debit. You may also have to pay a proportion of your profits.

INSURANCE

Public Liability

If you are hired as a freelancer to work in different venues and are paid on invoice (not as an employee), then you will need some sort of public liability insurance. This is usually inexpensive, but means that if someone breaks a leg during one of your workshops, you are covered. Some organizations will not hire you as a freelancer without this form of insurance.

Home Office

The moment you use any part of your home to conduct a business, it alters the use of your house, so you need different insurance. Several companies, realizing that millions of people now work regularly from home doing office-type work, offer specialist homeworker policies. Shop around. Often, they believe that all homeworkers have a trillion pounds' worth of equipment, rather than £300 worth of second-hand computer gear.

Car Insurance

There's a wonderful scene in Simon Armitage's book *All Points North*. He has just given up life as a social worker in order to work full-time as a poet. He informs his car insurer, who then insist that he has to pay additional premiums because poets are a higher risk than social workers.

If you make any income from writing, you will have to inform your car insurer that you now also write, even if on a part-time basis. For many people, this would mean that they might have to pay a higher insurance premium. This is because all writers are 100mph tailgating lunatics, who are probably out of their skulls on drink and drugs anyway. You just have to bite the bullet and pay up.

13 LOOKING AFTER YOURSELF

It's easy to think that writing is simply a desk job and that therefore there are no hazards. This isn't entirely true. You need to look after your health as a writer, both physically and mentally. There are dangers lurking in your home office, where you don't have the advantage of having a Health and Safety specialist on call (unless you happen to be one). Similarly, there are a lot of disadvantages to working alone.

THE DANGERS ON YOUR DESKTOP

Working at a computer is not in the same league as working on a building site or an oil rig, but it does have its dangers. It is not the computer in itself that is dangerous, but the way in which you use it when you sit there hacking out your *magnum opus*.

The way in which you sit, work and position your furniture and equipment is crucial. Eye strain, back and neck strain and Repetitive Strain Injury (RSI) are common problems and you need to set up your area of work so as to cut down on the possibility of any of these. They may seem like low-level complaints, but any of them can stop you working for weeks at a time, or cut your output to a trickle.

Getting the right set-up for your computer is vital. Your keyboard should be on the same horizontal plane as your wrists and directly in front of you. You should not use the surface of the desk as a rest for your wrists as you type. If you find you do this – a cause of carpal tunnel syndrome (a form of RSI) – consider buying a gel wrist pad. These cost only a few pounds – the foam versions are even cheaper – and it could be the best accessory you buy. If you type for long periods of time with your fingers held significantly higher than your wrists, you could end up with this painful disease. Similarly, if you find that you use your mouse for extended periods of time, you can get RSI from the little movements that are needed for manipulating a mouse. You can buy a mouse mat with a built-in gel-filled wrist roll.

Do not think that RSI is some kind of faddy, silly disease that is the invention of feckless office girls wanting time off to recover from a hangover. If you have ever come across anyone who has it, they will tell you it can be excruciatingly painful and can cause real, long-term problems. I am reliably informed that it is the second most common work-related disorder in the UK. (Apparently dermatitis is the most common, but I bet stress is rising fast.)

The height of your VDU (the monitor/screen) is also essential. The screen should be at approximately the same height as your eyes so that you are not craning your neck towards it. The monitor should also be directly in front of you and, if you are the kind of writer who writes longhand and then copytypes, it is best to have a copyholder that raises your work to the same height as the monitor. To avoid eye strain from glare, you might think about buying an anti-reflection screen. If you have got a flickering monitor, you must put it right. With equipment being so cheap nowadays, you can pick up a secondhand monitor for peanuts, especially if you have got the space for an old, chunky one.

Stop looking at your screen for a few minutes at least every half an hour. One way of combating this is to print out your work every so often and have a quick read of what you have done or, if you prefer, to have something put to one side that you have already written that needs checking. Then you can at least give your eyes a change of scene. Also, don't be frightened to give yourself proper breaks; if you are going to have a cup of tea or whatever, why not take it out into the garden on finer days and give yourself a few minutes to do some minor job there.

Back problems are rife amongst writers. Sitting is bad for the spine as it compresses it. In the manner of old-fashioned girls' schools, you have to think about posture. When you get up in the morning, your back has a kind of curve to it, so the spine is shaped like a loose 'S' or a sea horse. As the day progresses, the spine becomes more upright, until towards the end of the day, it can curve in the wrong direction, resembling a sort of 'C'. Sitting does not help. If the pressure on your spine is 100 per cent when you are standing, then lying down flat on your back exerts only 24 per cent pressure. Sitting with your back at an angle of 90 degrees to your thighs exerts a pressure of 140 per cent on the intervertebral discs; lean forward slightly, making the angle between thigh and back 80 degrees and you increase the pressure in your discs to 190 per cent.

When sitting for long periods of time either get a lumbar pillow, or failing that roll a towel into a cylinder and trap it in the small of your back. Physiotherapists' advice is to imagine you have a rope attached to the top of your head and someone is pulling it up. Keep your head in line with your shoulders and buttocks. Do not slouch. Obviously lying down is best, but unless you live in Hollywood it's hard to make a decent living on your back.

When working at your computer, it is best to keep your pelvis straight. If possible sit on a seat that slopes downwards slightly, so that your knees are below your hips. Like an opera singer, you should breathe from the diaphragm. Try to make small movements with your body whilst sitting. Rocking slightly may make you look even madder than you are, but it will at least increase the

> ### Your Personal Health-and-Safety Checklist for Working at a Computer
>
> There are Health and Safety regulations that will protect workers in companies, but you are on your own and responsible for your own health and welfare. Bad habits are easy to fall into. So, if you want a happy and productive life, look after yourself.
>
> - Is your desk stable?
> - Does your chair have five feet?
> - Can you adjust the seat back?
> - Does it support your back?
> - Can you adjust the height of the seat?
> - Do you feel any excess pressure on the underside of your thighs or on the backs of your knees?
> - Do your feet touch the floor? If not, do you have a foot rest?
> - Is there anything under your desk restricting the movement of your feet or legs?
> - Are your forearms more or less horizontal?
> - Are your wrists comfortable?
> - Do you have somewhere to rest your wrists during breaks from typing?
> - Is your head at a comfortable angle to the VDU?
> - Do you intersperse other tasks when you are using the computer?
> - Do you take a break from your computer every half an hour?

circulation to your body and greater blood flow helps concentration. Keep your feet on the floor and try to avoid crossing them. If you can't reach the floor, get a foot rest.

COPING WITH REJECTION

If those are the main physical effects of writing, there can also be psychological effects. Don't pooh-pooh these. Unless you are extremely resilient, writing can occasionally seem like an uphill battle.

Like many others before or since, anyone who writes has to learn to cope with rejection. As I write this section, I feel like the greatest hypocrite on Earth. I hate rejection; it is difficult to get used to it. However, over time you resign yourself to the fact that it will happen and you learn to live with it. Rejection hurts and the more of yourself, your time, energy, thought and passion that you put into something, the more it hurts. I do find that rejection is easier when it comes to non-fiction work than it is with imaginative writing. Perhaps there is just a little bit less of the author's soul in non-fiction than there is in works of the imagination.

There is, of course, one sure-fire way of avoiding rejection. If you don't send your work out in the first place, no one will reject it. It doesn't do your bank balance much good, though. A much better approach is to try to have as many ideas and proposals floating around publishers' and editors' offices as possible.

Of course, that makes you even more likely to be rejected, but it also increases your chances of acceptance. On the day Crowood accepted this book, I had a rejection from America on a historical article I was bursting to write. I hardly noticed the rejection – I'd had an acceptance.

You can minimize the risk of rejection by making sure that all those things that are within your control are done to the best of your ability. This includes:

- Making your writing as good as it possibly can be.
- Presenting your work in a professional manner.
- Making sure that you have provided the right product for the right market (as far as it is possible to tell) – the right length, the right style, the right approach and so on.

However, even if you have done extensive market research there may be factors that are completely beyond your control, such as:

- A magazine may already have a similar piece lined up.
- They use regular contributors only.
- They covered it too recently.
- There has been a change of editor or editorial policy.
- They simply don't take unsolicited material.

If you try to sell the idea, rather than the finished product, it always feels less hurtful when that idea comes bouncing back with a 'no thank you' message attached.

Sometimes, especially when you are starting out, you might get a near miss. Some magazines have pro forma checklists that they send out with their rejections. You can learn from this. Even more useful is the rejection slip that has a note that reads something like 'I liked this piece, but we already have this topic covered in our next issue.' A near miss is a good sign. It means that you are not being rejected for the quality of your writing. If you get a full letter, giving you an in-depth explanation, then try to get back to that editor with another idea; he or she likes your work and you should strike whilst the iron is hot.

The problem is that you will rarely receive an explanation for rejection, or if you do, it is a template letter that looks vaguely personal, because they've added your name and address. As a new writer, you may expect editors and publishers to take time out to tell you why they don't want your work. It would be great if they did, but unfortunately, that's not their job. They're busy people and they are only interested in manuscripts that might be of use to them. The result, as far as you are concerned, is that work is often rejected for no reason. You have no idea if it is any good or not.

Imagine you are going to have a conservatory built on your house. You invite half a dozen companies round to quote for the job. Eventually, you compare what they have to offer and make a decision. You then telephone that company and let them know you are going with them. The vast majority of people wouldn't even consider telephoning the 'losing' companies and certainly wouldn't write to explain why they didn't give them the job.

The same is true of editors. You might get a quick note that says something like 'We covered this a couple of years back'. What you are unlikely to get is a fulsome critique of why your work was rejected. You're not phoning round the conservatory companies to tell them why they didn't get the job, why should the editor explain to you? And arguing that you enclosed an SAE isn't going to help.

It's a tough world out there and there are enough people to put you off without my joining in. Treat editors and publishers in exactly the same way as you would God, only better. Then when they're nasty, treat them like the Devil incarnate. Fair's fair.

There's little consolation to be had in any of this. Possibly the only way to avoid feeling too upset by rejection is by having so many pitches and proposals on the go, that someone is bound to accept something. Even then, expect a cluster of rejections. Like the fallen rider getting back on the horse, rewrite your idea and send it out elsewhere.

What you have to try to do is to separate out the rejection from anything personal. It is not *you* who is being rejected, but your idea. One freelance writer I know tries to have fifty ideas with editors and publishers at any given time. I never seem to come up with enough ideas for that, but I admire the determination. And when you're not coping with rejection, then you have to cope with criticism.

As soon as you have anything published, you are fair game for all sorts of comments. Some people will like what you have written; some may even love it (and not all of them will necessarily be family). You have to treat good reviews and bad reviews with equal disdain. If you work on the principal that the critics are, in the words of Brendan Behan, 'like eunuchs in the harem, they've seen it all done every day, but they can't do it themselves,' then you'll feel a good deal better. Forget the critics if you can: they are a bunch of snivelling, self-righteous, boorish, oafish chumps who fancy themselves too clever to do the job that you are doing.

LOOKING AFTER YOUR PRECIOUS TIME

If you can put your rejections and criticisms to one side for a moment, you also need to be making sure that you are being productive. There's nothing more depressing than not finding the time to write or when you do, frittering it away tidying your pencil drawer. Organizing your time is one of the key ingredients to successful writing. Not only do you need to set aside time to write, but if your career takes off, even as a part-time career, you will find that you start to get competing pressures on your time.

It is important to try to make time for all the separate components of your writing. As a rule of thumb, you should always try to do a job when you get it. That way, it is out of your way, not looming over you like some Damoclesian sword and you can either get on with the rest of your life or cope with other work that comes in. The reality, however, is always a little different.

I try to have a four-tier priority system. It doesn't always work, but it enables me to feel organized. Essentially, it's just a posh to-do list, but it shows me what the most important tasks are:

Tier 1 – Important Stuff that Needs Doing Now

This, of course, will vary with what you are doing and the time of year. Typically this would be articles with approaching deadlines, my tax return, a pitch that if I don't send now will be out of date because it is time-sensitive or linked with an anniversary.

Tier 2 – Important Stuff with Longer Deadlines

This can soon become 'Important Stuff that Needs Doing Now', or even 'Important Stuff I Should Have Done Last Week' if you don't stay on top of it. Books are the most obvious example, although if you've sold a series of articles, editors often want them all together, so you need to be ticking these over on a regular basis.

Tier 3 – Stuff that Needs Doing to Keep Me in Work

This includes such items as answering emails from people who might buy articles, correspondence, or bookkeeping, pitches and proposals. A lot of this isn't particularly urgent, but if you don't do it, it can bog you down terribly. Besides, if you're not sending out pitches and proposals, then at some point you are going to find that you have a huge gap in your workload, and thus income. Keeping these bits and pieces under control is important, but they are items that can be put to one side if you suddenly have the pressure of a handful of deadlines coinciding.

Tier 4 – Unimportant Stuff

If you work in an office, you will be constantly interrupted by people in person, on the phone, via email. At home, you normally get far less of that, but you will find that you get more domestic interruptions instead. Do your utmost to ignore them.

JUGGLING ALL THOSE BALLS

Once you get going with writing different things, it can be hard to meet all the different demands. This puts a different kind of psychological pressure on you. One handy tip to keep you going is to intersperse bigger jobs with smaller ones. I think a lot of people's work stutters because they try to put their heads down and charge at the job. Often, working in short, but highly productive bursts works best. Don't be frightened to take breaks. Walk the dog for fifteen minutes; peel some potatoes for dinner; answer a letter that will only take a few minutes; do some neck-stretching exercises.

Let's suppose that your priority of the day is to write a 1,000-word article to rough, but you also need to be ticking over some other work. You also have a large project – a 50,000-word book with a deadline well in the future. It is important that you make some inroads into that article. If you don't do something about it, it will begin to loom larger and you will start to feel as though the weight of the world is on your shoulders. Starting work on it will at least make you feel as though you are making progress.

Your best bet is to start the day by working on the article. Write until you are beginning to flag, then when you get to the stage when you need to have a coffee to keep you going, do exactly that. Whilst you're taking a coffee break, there are bound to be some small jobs you can knock off – checking email or your post or doing five minutes' bookkeeping. Doing these sorts of fiddly jobs has the added advantage of enabling you to cross a couple of items off your to-do list.

After you've done that, then it is back to finishing the article. It's not unreasonable to be able to write a rough first draft of a 1,000-word article in two hours, possibly less. So, if you write it in two or three bursts of energy, you will find that you not only have your rough draft, but have also done a few other minor chores. However, you still have that book looming over you. Whenever you sign a book deal, the hand-in date is always well in the future. It is amazing how quickly the months become weeks and then days as that deadline looms.

The only way to deal with a big job like that is to nibble off chunks of it daily; break it up into manageable segments. Otherwise, you will suddenly find that you have not left yourself enough time to do the job. Then, you will not only feel under enormous pressure, but possibly even out of control as well. You can end up doing little bits of lots of jobs in a frantic fire-fighting, rearguard action against your growing to-do list and end up achieving nothing.

When you have several articles to write and a couple of books commissioned, you can certainly start feeling as though you're making something of a success of your writing. However, you now have different demands on your time. If you're also holding down a part-time or full-time job and/or have family commitments, it gets even harder.

For the jobbing non-fiction writer, one of the biggest difficulties is the common complaint of many small businesses: that it's either famine or feast. Either you have got plenty of work with looming deadlines, or no one seems to want anything from you. You need to be sending out ideas and proposals all the time or your work will eventually dry up. If you have got plenty of work with tight deadlines, it's often difficult to create the time needed to keep new work rolling in.

COPING WITH SOLITUDE

If you go out to work, the chances are you are in an environment where you are meeting other people. There is the chance to chat, to gossip, to share opinions about last night's TV, to find out if a film or a play is worth going to see, or to hear the latest woes about the local football team. When you work from home, it is great that you're not spending time commuting to work. It is great that you don't have to deal with the latest machinations of over-promoted managers and office politics. However, there is no doubt that you do miss the chit-chat by the water cooler.

There are times for many of us when, instead of feeling liberated by work-ing and living in the same place, we feel trapped by it. When you start writing full-time, because so much of the business of writing is conducted via email or post, sometimes the phone may not ring for days. When it does ring, you will inevitably get a cluster of calls on the day when you have got three deadlines and a computer that has taken to sulking and switching itself off automati-cally, and the last thing you want is yet more interruptions.

If you don't meet other people in the course of your writing, you can, of course, seek solace in your local pub. It's a good way to while away a couple of hours, but if you don't know anyone, it could be a recipe for alcoholism and penury. Try to make sure that you see plenty of friends: take up invitations to events, parties, concerts and plays. Go to an evening class, take up a sport or join a club. If you're musical, start a band or join a choir. Join an amateur drama group, go to church; in short, find something that will bring you into contact with other people.

Writers' circles are another option. In fact, you could always start your own. They can be a good idea, especially if you see your non-fiction writing as a means of helping you to develop your imaginative writing and what you take to your circle is that, rather than your money-making work.

A good writers' circle can encourage people to produce excellent work. It is also a way of ensuring that you are producing something new each week. However, too many fall into the trap of becoming biscuit-eating clubs, or one person's hobby horse, or forums where no genuine criticism takes place, or worse still, forums where cold-blooded critical assassination is the order of the day.

If you can find a circle that suits you, it might be a way of meeting others (on the other hand, it is still to do with writing and you might just fancy a com-plete change). They can help when they are genuinely encouraging. This is especially true when you've had a rejection letter. You can take it to the group and let off steam.

Remember, as a writer, you are the most important piece of machinery in your organization and if you break down, the whole kit and caboodle grinds to a halt.

USEFUL INFORMATION

CREATIVE WRITING BOOKS FOR NON-FICTION AUTHORS

Baverstock, A., *Marketing Your Book – an Author's Guide* (A&C Black, 2001).
Buzan, T., *How to Mind-Map* (HarperCollins, 2002).
Corder, N., *Writing Your Own Life Story* (Straightforward Publishing, 2004).
Crofts, A., *The Freelance Writer's Handbook* (Piatkus, 2002).
Dial, C., *Teach Yourself Travel Writing* (Teach Yourself Books, 2001).
Dick, J., *Freelance Writing for Newspapers* (A&C Black, 2003).
Dick, J., *Writing for Magazines* (A&C Black, 1996).
Dorner, J., *The Internet – A Writer's Guide* (A&C Black, 2000).
Field, M., *The Writer's Guide to Research* (How To Books, 2000).
Forche, C. and Gerrard, P. (eds), *Writing Creative Non-Fiction* (Writer's Digest Books, 2001).
Haynes, A., *Writing Successful Textbooks* (A&C Black, 2001).
Hoffmann, A., *Research for Writers* (A&C Black, 2003).
Keeble, R. (ed.), *The Newspapers Handbook* (Routledge, 2001).
Larsen, M., *How to Write a Book Proposal* (Writer's Digest Books, 2004).
Legat, M., *Writing for a Living* (A&C Black, 2000).
McCallum, C., *The Writers' Guide to Getting Published* (How To Books, 2003).
McKay, J., *The Magazines Handbook* (Routledge, 2000).
Ralph, J., *Teach Yourself the Internet for Writers* (Teach Yourself Books, 2001).
Scott, K., *The Internet Writer's Handbook* (Allison & Busby, 2001).
Wade, S., *A Straightforward Guide to Freelance Writing* (Straightforward Publishing, 1999).

USEFUL BOOKS FOR BUSINESS WRITING

Bartram, P., *How to Write a Press Release* (How To Books, 1995).
Baverstock, A., *Publicity, Newsletters and Press Releases* (Oxford University Press, 2002).
Patten, D., *Successful Marketing for the Small Business* (Kogan Page, 1989).
Wimbs, D., *Freelance Copywriting* (A&C Black, 1999).

BOOKS ON TEACHING

Corder, N., *Learning to Teach Adults – An Introduction* (RoutledgeFalmer, 2002).
   OK, so I'm plugging my own book here. It was written for people with little experience of teaching adults and is a general primer. It is an accessible, straightforward read rather than an academic textbook. You might find it useful to read before going on to look at materials that are aimed specifically at teaching writing.

O'Rourke, R. and Robinson, M., *Running Good Writing Groups* (NAWG Publications, 2003).
   This is an excellent resource pack that includes ideas for how to get your group going and also ideas for different writing activities. It is available directly from NAWG, The Arts Centre, Biddick Lane, Washington, Tyne and Wear NE38 2AB (UK).

MARKET GUIDES AND SOURCES FOR WRITERS

The Writers' and Artists' Yearbook (A&C Black, published annually).
The Writer's Handbook (Macmillan, published annually).
Willings Press Guide (Hollis Directories, published annually).

REFERENCE BOOKS

Everyone has their own preferred reference books. I suggest that a minimum requirement is something along these lines:

- A good-quality thesaurus.
- A large single-volume English dictionary.
- Burchfield, R.W., *Fowler's Modern English Usage* (Oxford University Press, 2004).
- A world atlas.
- *Whitaker's Almanac* (published annually).
- A good single-volume encyclopaedia, such as *Pears Cyclopaedia* (Penguin Books Ltd, published annually).
- *Brewer's Dictionary of Phrase and Fable* (Avon Books, 2000).
- A good book of quotations. *The Oxford Dictionary of Quotations* (Oxford University Press) is excellent.
- *On This Day* or an equivalent publication that gives details of anniversaries and so on.
- *Who's Who* is also useful if you are going to be dealing with well-known personalities or the great and the good.
- *The Penguin Dictionary of Clichés* (2000) – if it's in there, try not to use it.
- Gowers, Sir E., *Complete Plain Words* (Penguin Books Ltd 1987).
- Bryson, B., *Bryson's Dictionary of Troublesome Words: A Writer's Guide to Getting it Right* (Broadway Books, 2004).

SITES FOR SERIOUS RESEARCHERS

- The British Library is at *www.bl.uk*. You can click through from here to the Newspaper Library.
- Questia (*www.questia.com*) is an online library specializing in books and journals in the humanities and social sciences. It is a subscription service, although some books are available as a sample free of charge. You can take out an annual or monthly subscription.

MAGAZINES FOR WRITERS

There are several magazines on the market for the freelance writer.

The New Writer. A useful magazine, which prints short stories that have been short-listed for the Ian St James award, as well as useful articles on how to get your work published and writing-related issues. Also prints details of competitions, what's new, and so on, and has an email update for subscribers. (PO Box 60, Cranbrook, Kent TN17 2ZR, UK; *www.thenewwriter.com*)

Writers' News. A general pot pourri of information for the newer writer, including market news, opinion columns, short stories and so forth. The same publishers also produce *Writing Magazine*. (*Writer's News* and *Writing Magazine*, 1st Floor, Victoria House, 142–145 The Headrow, Leeds, LS1 5RL; *www.writersnews.co.uk*)

Writers' Forum. This is a similar sort of publication to *Writers' News*, available from news stands. (Writers International, PO Box 3229, Bournemouth, BH1 1ZS, UK; *www.writers-forum.com*)

Freelance Market News. A slim publication, which gives targeted information about magazines open to pitches from freelancers. (The Association of Freelance Writers, Sevendale House, 7 Dale Street, Manchester, M1 1JB, UK; *www.writersbureau.com*)

USEFUL INFORMATION

USEFUL WEBSITES FOR WRITERS

www.journalismuk.co.uk
www.freelanceuk.com
www.mediauk.com

On this Day, Births and Deaths Websites
www.historychannel.com
www.scopesys.com – This is actually an electronics repair company, but for some reason they have an 'on this day' section.

Late Payment
www.payontime.co.uk

Computers and Technical
OpenOffice software can be downloaded from the Sun Microsystems site at *www.sun.com*.

Voice Recognition Software
The two brand leaders are IBM Viavoice and Dragon Naturally Speaking.

MAGAZINES THAT TAKE FILLERS

This is not an exhaustive list, but try: *Bella, Best, Chat, My Weekly, Readers' Digest, Take a Break, That's Life, Woman's Own, Woman's Weekly,* and *Yours.*

COURSES FOR WRITERS

To find a course in your area, try your local adult education centre or further education college. You might also find LearnDirect (*www.learndirect.co.uk*) useful, especially as it lists correspondence courses.

If you want to go into journalism on a serious level, specific journalism courses are widely available. *Try* the National Council for the Training of Journalists (*www.nctj.com*).

For short courses, try the Adult Residential Colleges Association. The member colleges of this group hold all sorts of different courses throughout the country, mostly in comfortable surroundings with good food. Several run writing courses, which can include writing non-fiction. The ARCA Secretary is at 6 Bath Road, Felixstowe, Suffolk IP11 7JW, UK; *www.arca.uk.net.*

Arvon Foundation
The Arvon Foundation is a specialist provider of courses for writers at all levels. (National Office: 42a Buckingham Palace Road, London SW1W 0RE, UK; *www.arvonfoundation.org*) They have centres in various locations in the country:

Lumb Bank. (The Ted Hughes Arvon Centre, Heptonstall, Hebden Bridge, West Yorkshire HX7 6DF, UK; tel: 01422 843714.)

Moniack Mhor. (Teavarran, Kiltarlity, Beauly, Inverness-shire IV4 7HT, UK; tel: 01463 741675.)

The Hurst. (The John Osborne Arvon Centre, Clunton, Craven Arms Shropshire SY7 0JA, UK; tel: 01588 640658.)

Totleigh Barton. (Sheepwash, Beaworthy, Devon EX21 5NS, UK; tel: 01409 231338.)

Open College of the Arts
www.oca-uk.com

National Extension College
www.nec.ac.uk

TALKS

The following organizations sometimes hire speakers. Check your library for local groups: Inner Wheel, Lion's Club, Mothers' Union, National Women's Register, Probus, Rotary Club, Soroptomists, Townswomen's Guild, University of the Third Age, and the Women's Institute.

Greetings Cards

- *Greetings*, the magazine of the Greeting Card Association can be found at *www.greetingcardassociation.org.uk*.
- Yahoo's link for greetings cards manufacturers is: *http://dir.yahoo.com/ Business_and_Economy/Shopping_and_Services/Gifts_and_Occasions/ Greeting_Cards/*.

Organizations of Use to Writers

Public Lending Right. PLR pass on fees from libraries to authors of books. (Richard House, Sorbonne Close, Stockton-on-Tees, TS17 6DA, UK; tel: 01642 604699; *www.plr.uk.com*)

Authors' Licensing and Collecting Society. ALCS passes on photocopying and other fees to writers of magazine articles and books. (Marlborough Court, 14–18 Holborn, London EC1N 2LE, UK; tel: 0207 395 0600; *www.alcs.co.uk*)

National Union of Journalists. The NUJ is the foremost organization for freelance writers selling to newspapers and magazines. They have negotiated rates with various employers, although unfortunately most magazines simply do not pay NUJ rates. They also advise free-lance writers to negotiate the best deals they can. There are reduced rates for people not earning a huge amount from journalism.

The NUJ publishes useful guides on many issues affecting freelance writers and can help you pursue your case against non-payers. (NUJ, Headland House, 308–312 Gray's Inn Road, London WC1X 8DB, UK; tel: 020 7278 7916; *www.nuj.org.uk*)

The London freelance branch of the NUJ also has a useful website at *www.londonfreelance.org.uk*.

Society of Authors. The organization for professional writers, with lots of benefits available to members. You have to have had a certain number of items published in order to join. (84, Drayton Gardens, London SW10 9SB, UK; *www.societyofauthors.net*)

National Association of Writers in Education. NAWE is open to anyone interested in writing in education. There are no qualifications to join and their annual subscription fee is low. They publish a magazine, *Writing in Education*, and also have lots of useful information on their website at *www.nawe.co.uk*.

Useful Websites for Second-Hand Books

- *www.abe.com*
- *www.abebooks.com*
- *www.alibris.com*
- *www.bibliodirect.com*
- *www.biblion.co.uk*
- *www.bookfinder.com*
- *www.booklovers.co.uk*
- *www.glynsbooks.co.uk*

INDEX